# First World War
### and Army of Occupation
# War Diary
### France, Belgium and Germany

34 DIVISION
102 Infantry Brigade,
Brigade Machine Gun Company
25 April 1916 - 31 January 1918

WO95/2463/7

The Naval & Military Press Ltd
www.nmarchive.com
**Published in association with The National Archives**

Published by

The Naval & Military Press Ltd

Unit 10 Ridgewood Industrial Park,

Uckfield, East Sussex,

TN22 5QE England

Tel: +44 (0) 1825 749494

www.naval-military-press.com

www.nmarchive.com

*This diary has been reprinted in facsimile from the original. Any imperfections are inevitably reproduced and the quality may fall short of modern type and cartographic standards.*

© **Crown Copyright**
**Images reproduced by permission of The National Archives, London, England, 2015.**

# Contents

| Document type | Place/Title | Date From | Date To |
|---|---|---|---|
| Heading | WO95/2463 34 Division 102 Infantry Brigade Brigade Machine Gun Company April 1916-Jan 1918 | | |
| Heading | 34th Division 102nd Infy Bde 102nd Machine Gun Coy. Apr 1916-Jan 1918 | | |
| War Diary | Grantham | 25/04/1916 | 25/04/1916 |
| War Diary | Southampton | 25/04/1916 | 25/04/1916 |
| War Diary | Havre | 26/04/1916 | 27/04/1916 |
| War Diary | St. Omer | 27/04/1916 | 27/04/1916 |
| War Diary | St. Martin | 27/04/1916 | 28/04/1916 |
| War Diary | Muncqnieurlet | 29/04/1916 | 05/05/1916 |
| War Diary | St Omer Long ? (Amiens) | 06/05/1916 | 06/05/1916 |
| War Diary | St. Gratien | 07/05/1916 | 10/05/1916 |
| War Diary | Franvillers | 11/05/1916 | 31/05/1916 |
| Heading | 102 M.G. Coy War Diary for month of June 1916. Vol 2. | | |
| War Diary | Franvillers | 01/06/1916 | 02/06/1916 |
| War Diary | Albert | 03/06/1916 | 30/06/1916 |
| Heading | 102nd Bde. 34th Div. War Diary 102nd Machine Gun Company July 1916. | | |
| War Diary | Albert | 26/06/1916 | 04/07/1916 |
| War Diary | Millencourt | 06/07/1916 | 14/07/1916 |
| War Diary | Liencourt | 15/07/1916 | 16/07/1916 |
| War Diary | Fosse De La Claronel | 17/07/1916 | 25/07/1916 |
| War Diary | Villers Au Bois | 26/07/1916 | 31/07/1916 |
| Heading | 102nd Brigade 37th Division till 21.8.16 34th Division from 22.8.16 102th Brigade Machine Gun Company August 1916 | | |
| War Diary | Villers Au Bois | 01/08/1916 | 18/08/1916 |
| War Diary | Estrce Couche | 19/08/1916 | 19/08/1916 |
| War Diary | Frevillers | 20/08/1916 | 20/08/1916 |
| War Diary | Trevincourt | 21/05/1916 | 26/05/1916 |
| War Diary | Armentieres | 26/05/1916 | 30/11/1916 |
| Heading | War Diary Dec 1916. 102 M.G. Coy. Vol 8. | | |
| War Diary | Armentieres | 01/12/1916 | 12/12/1916 |
| War Diary | Erquinghem | 13/12/1916 | 15/12/1916 |
| War Diary | Erquinghem | 14/12/1916 | 23/12/1916 |
| War Diary | Armentieres | 23/12/1916 | 27/01/1917 |
| War Diary | Mereten | 28/01/1917 | 28/01/1917 |
| War Diary | Caestre | 28/01/1917 | 31/01/1917 |
| Heading | War Diary of 102nd Machine Gun Company. Month-February, 1917. Vol 10. | | |
| War Diary | Caestre | 01/02/1917 | 18/02/1917 |
| War Diary | Morbecque | 19/02/1917 | 19/02/1917 |
| War Diary | Mazingham | 20/02/1917 | 20/02/1917 |
| War Diary | Guestreville | 21/02/1917 | 21/02/1917 |
| War Diary | Ecoivres | 22/02/1917 | 23/02/1917 |
| War Diary | Arras | 23/02/1917 | 08/03/1917 |
| War Diary | Ecoivres | 08/03/1917 | 09/03/1917 |
| War Diary | Dieval | 10/03/1917 | 20/03/1917 |
| War Diary | Bethonsart | 21/03/1917 | 21/03/1917 |

| Type | Description | Start | End |
|---|---|---|---|
| War Diary | Louez | 22/03/1917 | 31/03/1917 |
| Heading | War Diary April 1917 102nd Machine Gun Company. Vol 12. | | |
| War Diary | Louez | 01/04/1917 | 04/04/1917 |
| War Diary | Ecoivres | 05/04/1917 | 09/04/1917 |
| War Diary | Y Huts | 10/04/1917 | 15/04/1917 |
| War Diary | La Thieuloye | 16/04/1917 | 21/04/1917 |
| War Diary | ACQ | 22/04/1917 | 22/04/1917 |
| War Diary | Laressett | 23/04/1917 | 23/04/1917 |
| War Diary | Arras | 24/04/1917 | 30/04/1917 |
| Diagram etc | Diagram of Saps. used for special Barrage 102 M.G. Coy. Appendix I. | | |
| Miscellaneous | Certificate To Be Signed before Fire is Opened. | | |
| Diagram etc | 102 M.G. Sketch Showing Machine Gun Barrage from 6.30 am to 12 noon 9/4/17. Appendix II. | | |
| Miscellaneous | Appendix III | | |
| War Diary | | 01/05/1917 | 08/05/1917 |
| War Diary | Autheux | 09/05/1917 | 31/05/1917 |
| War Diary | St Nicholas | 01/06/1917 | 21/06/1917 |
| War Diary | Buneville | 22/06/1917 | 30/06/1917 |
| Map | Part of Sheet 51B N.W. Map. "A" attached to War Diary June 1917. 102 M.G. Coy. | | |
| Miscellaneous | Programme of Fire For No 4. Gun. Appendix B. | | |
| Miscellaneous | Instructions re Barrage Guns. Appendix C. | 04/06/1917 | 04/06/1917 |
| Miscellaneous | Orders for Gun Members Oc. Appendix C | 04/06/1917 | 04/06/1917 |
| Miscellaneous | Programme of Training for week ending 30/6/17. 102 M.G. Coy. Appendix D. | 23/06/1917 | 23/06/1917 |
| War Diary | Buneville | 01/07/1917 | 05/07/1917 |
| War Diary | Hamelet | 06/07/1917 | 14/07/1917 |
| War Diary | | 13/07/1917 | 19/07/1917 |
| War Diary | | 18/07/1917 | 21/07/1917 |
| War Diary | | 20/07/1917 | 26/07/1917 |
| War Diary | | 25/07/1917 | 27/07/1917 |
| War Diary | | 26/07/1917 | 27/07/1917 |
| War Diary | Bernes | 27/07/1917 | 05/08/1917 |
| War Diary | A Section 34 Divn. | 05/08/1917 | 08/08/1917 |
| War Diary | A Section 34 Divn. III Corps. | 08/08/1917 | 12/08/1917 |
| War Diary | Bernes | 12/08/1917 | 13/08/1917 |
| War Diary | B Section 34 Divn. | 13/08/1917 | 15/08/1917 |
| War Diary | B Section | 15/08/1917 | 18/08/1917 |
| War Diary | B Section 34 Divn. | 17/08/1917 | 28/08/1917 |
| War Diary | B Section | 28/08/1917 | 31/08/1917 |
| Miscellaneous | Appendix "A" to War Diary Vol XVII Aug 1917 of No 102 M.G. Coy. | | |
| Miscellaneous | Appendix A Contd. P II. | | |
| Map | Appendix B to War Diary Vol XVII Aug 1917 of 102 M.G. Coy. | | |
| Miscellaneous | Appendix C. to War Diary Vol XVII Aug 1917 of no. 102 M.G. Coy. | 26/08/1917 | 26/08/1917 |
| War Diary | | 01/09/1917 | 09/09/1917 |
| War Diary | | 08/09/1917 | 12/09/1917 |
| War Diary | | 11/09/1917 | 23/09/1917 |
| War Diary | | 22/09/1917 | 30/09/1917 |
| War Diary | Bellacourt | 01/10/1917 | 08/10/1917 |
| War Diary | Pegwell Camp-Proven | 09/10/1917 | 31/10/1917 |
| Miscellaneous | Distribution Statement. Appendix II. | | |

| | | | |
|---|---|---|---|
| War Diary | Saulty. | 07/10/1917 | 07/10/1917 |
| War Diary | Beaumetz. | 07/10/1917 | 07/10/1917 |
| War Diary | Gouy. | 07/10/1917 | 07/10/1917 |
| War Diary | Saulty | 07/10/1917 | 07/10/1917 |
| War Diary | Beaumetz. | 07/10/1917 | 07/10/1917 |
| War Diary | Gouy. | 07/10/1917 | 07/10/1917 |
| War Diary | Saulty. | 07/10/1917 | 07/10/1917 |
| War Diary | Beaumetz. | 07/10/1917 | 07/10/1917 |
| War Diary | Gouy. | 07/10/1917 | 07/10/1917 |
| War Diary | Beaumetz. | 07/10/1917 | 07/10/1917 |
| War Diary | Gouy. | 07/10/1917 | 07/10/1917 |
| War Diary | Saulty. | 07/10/1917 | 07/10/1917 |
| War Diary | Beaumetz. | 07/10/1917 | 07/10/1917 |
| War Diary | Gouy. | 07/10/1917 | 07/10/1917 |
| War Diary | Saulty | 07/10/1917 | 07/10/1917 |
| War Diary | Beaumetz. | 08/10/1917 | 08/10/1917 |
| War Diary | Gouy. | 08/10/1917 | 08/10/1917 |
| War Diary | Saulty. | 08/10/1917 | 08/10/1917 |
| War Diary | Beaumetz. | 08/10/1917 | 08/10/1917 |
| War Diary | Gouy. | 08/10/1917 | 08/10/1917 |
| War Diary | Beaumetz. | 08/10/1917 | 08/10/1917 |
| War Diary | Gouy. | 08/10/1917 | 08/10/1917 |
| War Diary | | 01/11/1917 | 30/11/1917 |
| War Diary | | 18/11/1917 | 01/12/1917 |
| War Diary | | 02/11/1917 | 02/11/1917 |
| War Diary | | 03/12/1917 | 04/12/1917 |
| War Diary | | 04/11/1917 | 10/11/1917 |
| War Diary | | 10/12/1917 | 31/01/1918 |

(7)

WO 95/2463

34 Division
102 Infantry Brigade
Brigade Machine Gun Company

April 1916 - Jan 1918

34TH DIVISION
102ND INFY BDE

102ND MACHINE GUN COY.
APR 1916-JAN 1918

34TH DIVISION
102ND INFY BDE

Army Form C. 2118.

102 MG

XXXIV

# WAR DIARY or INTELLIGENCE SUMMARY

*(Erase heading not required.)*

Instructions regarding War Diaries and Intelligence Summaries are contained in F.S. Regs., Part II. and the Staff Manual respectively. Title Pages will be prepared in manuscript.

| Place | Date | Hour | Summary of Events and Information | Remarks and references to Appendices |
|---|---|---|---|---|
| Grantham | 25/4/16 | 2.45 AM | Entrained & left Grantham station. | |
| Southampton | 25/4/16 | 11.30 AM | Arrived Southampton. | |
| | | 2.30 p.m | Company embarked – two transports. | |
| Havre | 26/4/16 | 5.5 AM | "   disembarked. No.12907 Pte Cocker left in hospital. | |
| | | 10 p.m | A + B Sections entrained | Apr '16 |
| | 27/4/16 | 3.30 AM | C + D   "       " } No. 13667 Private Shuttles kicked from train by mule | Dec '17 |
| | | 8.30 pm | A + B   "  arrived & de-trained } horse & admitted to hospital at Boulogne | |
| St Omer | – | 11.30 M | C + D   "    "    "    "  } | |
| St Martin | – | 12.30 pm | Company in billets. } Seen reported out of action due to broken knee spring – no spares available. | |
| | 2/4/16 | | Inspected by S.O.C. 34th Division | |
| | 3/4/16 | 3.30 pm | 13063 Pte Harrison 9. admitted to hospital in St Omer | |
| MUNCQ – NIEURLET | 29/4/16 | 11 AM | Company left in motor buses for new billet in Notre Dame Farm Muncq Nieurlet arriving about 2 p.m. } Water supply scarce & bad. | |
| – | 30/4/16 | 3 AM | Company left for Divisional field day returning 3 p.m. | |
| – | 1/5/16 | | Company raid. No 15549 Pte Gillott admitted to hospital in St Omer | |
| – | 2/5/16 | 3 AM | Company left for Divisional field day returning 2 p.m. | |
| – | 3/5/16 | 6 AM | "   "   "   "   "   "   " | |
| – | 4/5/16 | | Gas helmet drill & inspection | |
| – | 5/5/16 | 1.30 pm | Company marched to St Omer station & entrained. No 15609. Pte Russell admitted to hospital | |
| St Omer Long Pre AUT (Amiens) | 6/5/16 | 6.45 pm | Left St Omer station. | |
| | | 6 AM | " de-trained & marched to billets in St Gratien. | |
| St Gratien | 7/5/16 | | " resting. Horse found belonging A.S.C. Hoof mark 113. | |
| | 8/4/16 | 10 AM | " inspected by G.O.C. 102 Brigade. Horse claimed by A.S.C. | |

Army Form C. 2118.

# WAR DIARY
## or
## INTELLIGENCE SUMMARY
(Erase heading not required.)

Instructions regarding War Diaries and Intelligence Summaries are contained in F. S. Regs., Part II. and the Staff Manual respectively. Title Pages will be prepared in manuscript.

| Place | Date | Hour | Summary of Events and Information | Remarks and references to Appendices |
|---|---|---|---|---|
| St Gratien | 9/5/16 | | Gun drill. Company raid. | |
| | 10/5/16 | 6.30 pm | Company left St Gratien for Franvillers | |
| | 11/5/16 | 9.9 pm | " arrived & billeted in Franvillers | |
| Franvillers | 11/5/16 | | " drilled with gas helmets by M.O. | |
| " | 12/5/16 | | do | |
| " | 13/5/16 | | do    No 18609 Pte Russell returned to duty | |
| " | 14/5/16 | | do    developed Scabies. No 10484 Pte Bennett J. to No 36. C.C.S. | |
| " | 15/5/16 | | do    bathed in creosol. Straw in billets burned. | |
| " | 16/5/16 | | do    Gun drill mechanism etc | |
| " | 17/5/16 | | do    received hot bath. C.O. & 2/Lt Rutherford visited trenches | |
| " | 18/5/16 | | do    Gun drill etc Company raid. Company clear of Scabies. | |
| " | 19/5/16 | | do    C.O. Lt Moffatt & 2/Lt Moffatt visited trenches | |
| " | 20/5/16 | | do    C.O. visited trenches  Company raid. | |
| Franvillers | 20/5/16 | | Gun drill etc. | |
| | 21/5/16 | | do    etc. | |
| | 22/5/16 | | do    Lieut Murfitt & L/C Wisbey No 449 & left for transport course at Hesdin | |
| | 23/5/16 | | do    & bathed | |
| | 24/5/16 | | do    2.Lt Whitehouse, 2.Lt Piddock & 2.Lt Preston visited trenches. 6.6 N.C.O's & men from 102nd Brigade attached. No's 10585 Pte O'Neill D, 12629 Pte Scanlon J, 9085 Pte Roberts B, 9431 Pte Joyce J, 17630 Pte Smith G, 10578 Pte Morgan R, 3520 Pte Skreene J, 9141 Pte Baily R Posted to Company from base depot. No 65811 Pte Morgood J.J. R.A.M.C. attached for training | |

Army Form C. 2118.

# WAR DIARY
or
## INTELLIGENCE SUMMARY
(Erase heading not required.)

| Place | Date | Hour | Summary of Events and Information | Remarks and references to Appendices |
|---|---|---|---|---|
| FRANVILLERS | 25/5/16 | | Company Gun Drill &c. Company Raid | |
| " | 26/5/16 | | do | |
| " | 27/5/16 | | do C.O. 227 ROBSON & 227 WILLIAMS revisited trenches. | |
| " | 28/5/16 | | Company parade & billet inspection | |
| " | 29/5/16 5 a.m. | | Company left for Divisional manoeuvres returning 10.30 a.m. Gun out of action again reported to B.O.E. H.Q. | |
| " | 30/5/16 | | Company Gun Drill etc. No 10497 Pte WILSON to No 36 C.C.S. | |
| " | 31/5/16 | | do No 9946 Pte POWELL E.C. ) Posted from<br>No 1000 Pte RONALD J.W. ) Base Depot<br>No 3512 Pte PEACHMENT J. )<br>No 14160 Pte MIDGLEY J. ) | |

N.C. Ingham Capt.
Comdg 102nd Machine Gun Company.

102 MG Coy
Second offum
XXXIV
Vol 2

102nd M.G. Coy.

War Diary

for month of

June 1916

# WAR DIARY
## or
## INTELLIGENCE SUMMARY

Army Form C. 2118.

| Place | Date | Hour | Summary of Events and Information | Remarks and references to Appendices |
|---|---|---|---|---|
| FRANVILLERS | 1/6/16 | 6.5 A.M. | Company left for Divisional manoeuvres returning 9.30 A.M. | |
| | 2/6/16 | | Paid. | |
| | | | Left FRANVILLERS for ALBERT arriving 11.45 P.M. | |
| ALBERT. | 3/4/16 | 8 P.M. | A & B sections relieved two sections of No.101 Co in the line. | Refer Off No.1. |
| | | 4 A.M. | Heavy bombardment commenced against our lines. | Ref Off No 2 |
| | 4/6/16 | 12 MID.N | Enemy raided our trenches. No 1 PTE BALL J.R. slight bullet wound in neck. | |
| | | 1.30 A.M. | Heavy artillery bombardment commenced on both sides. | |
| | | 9 P.M. | Raid intended by B Co on our right forestalled by counter raid on part of enemy partly on our front & partly on front of B Co on right. It was noted that our guns were largely responsible for total eclipse of raid. The morale of the men on both these occasions their first under fire, was excellent. | |
| | 5/6/16 | 11 P.M. | After heavy bombardment commencing 11 P.M. a successful raid was carried out from our trenches under cover of a heavy barrage of machine gun fire directed against enemy Second & Third Line. | |
| | 6/6/16 | | Day & night quiet. Damage caused by bombardment repaired. | |
| | 7/6/16 | | Situation normal. | |
| | 8/6/16 | 4 A.M. | A & B sections relieved by C & D sections respectively. | |
| | 9/6/16 | | Situation normal ⎤ A certain amount of indirect fire carried out by day | |
| | 10/6/16 | | " ⎪ by two guns in Ilona Redoubt against enemy | |
| | 11/6/16 | | " ⎬ communication trenches. | |
| | 12/6/16 | | " ⎪ Two new emplacements commenced in MONYMUSK ST. | |
| | 13/6/16 | | " ⎦ | |

Army Form C. 2118.

# WAR DIARY
## or
## INTELLIGENCE SUMMARY

(Erase heading not required.)

| Place | Date | Hour | Summary of Events and Information | Remarks and references to Appendices |
|---|---|---|---|---|
| ALBERT | 10/6/16 | 4 a.m. | D Section on left relieved by B Section. 2 guns of C Section in DALHOUSIE ST. relieved by 2 guns of A Section. | Refer. App. No 1. |
| | | M.N. | 2 Right guns of C Section relieved by 101 M.G.Co. who from this date take over defence of right sector. | |
| | | 6 p.m. | Remaining 2 guns of A Section moved up to DALHOUSIE ST. Total number of guns now holding Divisional sector:- 6 of 102.M.G.C. on left & 2 of 101.M.G.C. on right. | |
| | 15/6/16 | | Further working parties from the 22nd Infantry were made to putting all 16 Burrows & the line. Sections which as before sweeping and working parties from training & lectures to assist the line, making new gun Emplacements and dug outs. | |
| | night of 19th | | No carrying parties were found as Setting was excluded from battle guns. Gas cylinders were carried to our front line. Enemy were frequent use of "Weai-stills". | |
| | 20/6/16 | 6 a.m. | C & D Sections relieved A & B Sections. C Section at Dalhousie Street. D at Mons Redoubt. (2 guns) and one gun each at St Andrews Avenue & Bray Street, and continued the improvements and new emplacements at Bray St. The St P. Andrews Avenue. | |
| | 23/6/16 | 4 noon | Remainder of Company H.Qrs came in trenches. H.Qrs also A & C Sections in Dalhousie. B Section at Bray Street, and D Section at Mons Redoubt & St Andrews Avenue. | |
| | 24/6/16 | 4a.m. 9 p.m. | Commencement of Days Bombardment. Gas attack covered by rapid fire from our guns, each firing at belt rapid. | |
| | 25/6/16 | | Bombardment continued; intermittently — firstly, large quantity of hostile shells falling offshore. | |

Army Form C. 2118.

# WAR DIARY
## or
## INTELLIGENCE SUMMARY
*(Erase heading not required.)*

Instructions regarding War Diaries and Intelligence Summaries are contained in F. S. Regs., Part II. and the Staff Manual respectively. Title Pages will be prepared in manuscript.

| Place | Date | Hour | Summary of Events and Information | Remarks and references to Appendices |
|---|---|---|---|---|
| ALBERT | 26/4/16 | | Smoke clouds sent over from our Trenches, M.G's 10 minutes Rapid fire | |
| | 27th | | | |
| | 28th | | Bombardment continued, little reply from enemy's guns. | |
| | 29 & 6/16 | | | |
| | 30 | | | |

J.B.Bradfiel
O.C. 102H.S.Coy

102nd Bde.
34th Div.

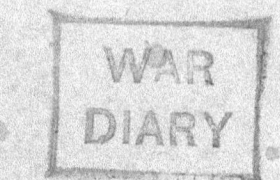

102nd MACHINE GUN COMPANY

JULY 1916.

# WAR DIARY or INTELLIGENCE SUMMARY

Army Form C. 2118.

102nd Machine Gun Coy

JULY

Vol 3

| Place | Date | Hour | Summary of Events and Information | Remarks and references to Appendices |
|---|---|---|---|---|
| ALBERT. | 26/6/16 | 6 p.m. | Smoke clouds sent over. M.Gs 10 minute rapid fire. | |
| | 27 | | | |
| | 28/6/16 | | | |
| | 29/6/16 | | Bombardment continues. Little reply from enemy's guns. | |
| | 30 | | | |
| | 1/7/16 | 6 a.m. | Intensive bombardment. Mine at La Boiselle exploded 7.28. Infantry & M.Gs advance 7.30. under very heavy machine gun and shrapnel fire. Most casualties caused by M.G bullets in legs. Front Coy: Capt. Ingpen kld. by shrapnel in back, afterwards Mr. Poolin "A" nearly shrapnel wound in neck, Mr. Paddock "C" after crossing front line killed by bullet in side. Mr. William "B" Shatteries knee cap, and Mr. Moffatt "B" bullet in thigh. Machine guns ordered to take up their original position. | |
| | | 9 a.m. | Suicide scouts to locate enemy's first & second lines. Towards evening took 3rd qu.h. Reinforced by 19th Division. Enemy's machine guns located in La Boiselle. Operations very active during night. 3 of Coy's guns lost out of 16. Guns after some men and guns buried but relocated. All men of the Coy showed great devotion to duty. | |
| | 2/7/16 | | 8th Division moved forward on left. La Boiselle bombed and many prisoners taken. By evening La Boiselle in our hands. 3 guns under Mr. Robson were forward into these Gali to hold same in case of Counter attack. Mr. Whitelaw "A" missing since morning of 1st. | |
| | 3/7/16 | | Troops progressed favourably both right and left. 3rd Division suffering heavily during advance. Gun teams in Gali not relieved owing 6 Coy moving our next day. M.G emplacements were found very unsuitable for rapid fire, owing to the Cordoli funds out "gaping" them for night firing, too often emplacements with not full screen in front were very suitable and none of the guns appear to have been spotted. | |
| | | | Note: During the above of advance (Gurne) | |

**Army Form C. 2118.**

# WAR DIARY
## or
## INTELLIGENCE SUMMARY
*(Erase heading not required.)*

Instructions regarding War Diaries and Intelligence Summaries are contained in F.S. Regs., Part II. and the Staff Manual respectively. Title Pages will be prepared in manuscript.

| Place | Date | Hour | Summary of Events and Information | Remarks and references to Appendices |
|---|---|---|---|---|
| Albert | 4/7/16 | 8am | Coy relieved, proceeded to Millencourt. Lieut Gibb, 2/Lieut Rutherford, 2/Lieut Robson, Sergt Smith, Callaghan, Ricketts, Cpls Cox, Morris and Sergeant transferred to 101st M.G. Coy. | |
| Millencourt | 6/4/16 | 6.30pm | Coy left in buses to La Bazeque, arrived 8am. 6/7/16. Received news of 2/Lt. Whitehurst severely wounded & missing from 2/Lt, at being in hospital in England, suffering from shell shock. Relit received from 21 N.I.D. M.Stat recommending Cpl DeLasso to D.C.M. heavy action taken though Bde. H. Qs Sergt of 30 men from Base & likely casualties | |
| do. | 7/4/16 | | Day of Rest | |
| | 8/7/16 | 9am | Overhauled h.b equipment. Cleaned guns. Coy had kit inspection | |
| | 9/4/16 | | Resuming lectures, general cleaning up of billets etc, washing of clothes. 6 officers reported for duty from Base to Relieve casualties | |
| | 10/7/16 | | Company bathing. Adopting of shirts. Physical section drill. Rifle exercises. Company parades. | |
| | 11/7/16 | | Company inspected by Divisional Commander. | |
| | 12/7/16 | | Physical section & gas helmet drill. Gun drill & instruction of Machine Gun. Orders received to England move tomorrow. | |
| | 13/7/16 | 3.30 | | |
| | 14/7/16 | 6pm | Company left La Bazeque and moved to Liencourt, arriving about 10.30pm Billeted in Barns to the right. | |

2449 Wt. W14957/M90 750,000 1/16 J.B.C. & A. Forms/C.2118/12.

Army Form C. 2118.

# WAR DIARY
## or
## INTELLIGENCE SUMMARY

(Erase heading not required.)

Instructions regarding War Diaries and Intelligence Summaries are contained in F. S. Regs., Part II and the Staff Manual respectively. Title Pages will be prepared in manuscript.

| Place | Date | Hour | Summary of Events and Information | Remarks and references to Appendices |
|---|---|---|---|---|
| Lierwort. | 15/7/16 | 9 p.m. | Left for Lucheville, arriving about 6.30 p.m. Billeted in bivvies for the night. | |
| | 16/7/16 | " | Left Lucheville and marched to Forêt de Lucheuvre arriving 1 p.m. Men comfortably billeted in huts. | |
| | 17/7/16 | | | |
| | | 6.30 A.M. | Coy. paraded for Physical Training. | |
| | | 9. A.M. } 12. Noon } | Coy. paraded for cleaning of guns, checking guns, kit inspection. | |
| | | 2. P.M. } 4. P.M. } | Gun drill, Mechanism and S.D.M. &c. | |
| Forêt De La Clavenet | 18/7/16 | | Coy resting at La Forêt de La Clavenet. Carried on with Coy Training, re-fitting the guns, and issuing new clothing. | |
| | 19/7/16 | | | |
| | 20/7/16 | | | |
| | 21/7/16 | | | |
| | 22/7/16 | | 1 Riding Horse to replace 1 horse evacuated by A.V.C. arrived. | |
| | 23/7/16 | | 1 Mule damaged by lying on a sharp object, gash on near side quarters. | |
| | 24/7/16 | | " Clothing" more No points. | |
| | 25/7/16 | | | |

**Army Form C. 2118.**

# WAR DIARY
## or
## INTELLIGENCE SUMMARY

*(Erase heading not required.)*

Instructions regarding War Diaries and Intelligence Summaries are contained in F. S. Regs., Part II. and the Staff Manual respectively. Title Pages will be prepared in manuscript.

| Place | Date | Hour | Summary of Events and Information | Remarks and references to Appendices |
|---|---|---|---|---|
| Villers au Bois | 26th | 9 A.M. | Coy Paraded to march to Villers-au-Bois, on arrival, A, B & C Sections relieved, A B & C Sections of 111st M.G. Coy. Relief complete at 2.30 A.M. 27th. | |
| " " | 27th Noon | | Intermittent shelling by Hostile guns, otherwise all quiet. Night was quiet, one of our own shells dropped near to Alhambra Emplacement, SP 1.30 alley. Hellements admitted into Hospital. | |
| " " | 29th " | | Pte 11648 Hine T. reported missing. All quiet on the line. No guns fired. | |
| " " | 30th " | | Hostile snipers, very busy on A30 alley (though the Zouave valley) Enemy made no movement during the night. Lewis guns in full go. | |
| " " | 31st " | | All quiet. Work being done on deepening and cleaning ours and new Emplacement under construction. | |

J.W. Shaw M.
O.C. 10R. M. G. Coy

2449 Wt. W14957/M90 - 750,000 1/16 J.B.C. & A. Forms/C.2118/12.

102nd Brigade

ATTACHED    37th Division till 21.8.16.

34th Division from 22.8.16.

-------------------

102th BRIGADE MACHINE GUN COMPANY

AUGUST 1 9 1 6 :::

Army Form C. 2118.

# WAR DIARY or INTELLIGENCE SUMMARY

102nd Machine Gun Coy.

Volume V

(Erase heading not required.)

| Place | Date | Hour | Summary of Events and Information | Remarks and references to Appendices |
|---|---|---|---|---|
| Villers au Bois | 1/8/16 | 9.A.M. | A Sect. in Front system relieved by 13 Sect. 1 Gun of D Sect. relieved 1 gun in "Ersatz" Trench of B Sect. C Sect. relieved B Sect. in Reserve system "Cabaret Rouge". | |
| " | 2/8/16 | " " | It is thought that an enemy relief took place a distinct difference in enemy tactics noticed, more artillery and trench mortar activity. Minenwerfers used freely from enemy trenches. | |
| " | 3/8/16 | " " | Pte. T. HOARE reported missing from "Stand To". Activity Normal, movement Nil. Increased hostile sniping activity, Pte Clements reported sick and evacuated. | |
| " | 4/8/16 | " " | Trench Mortar activity. Hostile sniping normal, Ration Dump moved to P.5. | |
| " | 5/8/16 | " " | C Sect relieved 13 Sect. Ersatz gun relieved by 1 gun of 1 sect. A sect. | |
| " | 6/8/16 | " " | relieved C Sect 2nd Lt. A.C. MILLS came back to rest in Villers au Bois, relieved by 2nd Lt. G. BELL. | |
| " | 7/8/16 | " " | Hostile activity normal, 2 enemy snipers reported killed. We also 1 MME on our sector, occupied by us. | |
| " | 8/8/16 | " " | Hostile activity Normal, Pte Gowling of Shrapnel wound in leg evacuated to C.C.S. | |
| " | 9/8/16 | " " | Activity Normal, one of our own shells fell near the ALHAMBRA Emplacement. Pte. Richardson, reported sick. SHELL SHOCK, Evacuated to C.C.S. | |
| " | 10/8/16 | " " | 103 M.G. Coy. relieved our Front system Implacements. and 3in Reserve system "Cabaret Rouge". We took over from them the "Bayete Vrie" & Sin left all was quiet on our Front. Work started on M.G Emplacement in Bay 52 "Souchez-Carency". R.E. material carried up. | |
| " | 11/8/16 | " " | Our 3 guns in Cabaret Rouge, relieved by 3 guns of 103 M.G. Coy. Relief complete by 12.20 M.M. | |

**Army Form C. 2118**

# WAR DIARY
## or
## INTELLIGENCE SUMMARY

*(Erase heading not required.)*

Instructions regarding War Diaries and Intelligence Summaries are contained in F. S. Regs., Part II. and the Staff Manual respectively. Title Pages will be prepared in manuscript.

| Place | Date | Hour | Summary of Events and Information | Remarks and references to Appendices |
|---|---|---|---|---|
| | 12/5/16 | | Coy in Reserve in Bayle Line, all quiet. | |
| | 13/5/16 | | " | |
| | 14/5/16 | | " | |
| | 15/5/16 | | " | |
| | 16/5/16 | | " | |
| | 17/5/16 | | " | |
| | 18/5/16 | | " | |
| | | Villers | Coy in Villers au-Bois, moved off 6.7 P.M. and billeted for the night | |
| | 19/5/16 | Bleu Couche | at Bleu Couche. | |
| | 20/5/16 | Frévillers | Coy marched to Frévillers, and comfortably billeted for the night. | |
| | 21/5/16 | " | " | |
| | 22/5/16 | Frévincourt | Coy in rest, after marching from Frévillers | |
| | 23/ 9/16 | | | |
| | 24/5/16 | | Coy training | |

Army Form C. 2118.

# WAR DIARY
## or
## INTELLIGENCE SUMMARY
*(Erase heading not required.)*

Instructions regarding War Diaries and Intelligence Summaries are contained in F. S. Regs., Part II. and the Staff Manual respectively. Title Pages will be prepared in manuscript.

| Place | Date | Hour | Summary of Events and Information | Remarks and references to Appendices |
|---|---|---|---|---|
| Turriwood | 25th | 9 A.M. | Bn marched off, and entrained at Bloré detrained at la Gorgue, thence by lorries to Armentières Transport entrained and billetted for the night at Inguingham. | |
| Armentières | 26th | 2 P.M. | lay in Trenches in Armentières sector. Relieved 12 guns of 54th M.G. Coy. | |
| Armentières | 27th | 9 A.M. | The day was quiet, slight hostile machine gun activity. | |
| " " | 28th | " | The day was normal, as of our aeroplanes returning from a raid two (1 at Boy hostile gun fire, and brought down within our lines. (more tak Apple) two more guns to be put into the the G.O.C.'s advanced H.Q. making 14 guns all told in our sector. 2nd Lt J. Rutherford admitted to hospital, also 2/Lt J. Halliday. | |
| " " | 29th | " | | |
| " " | 30th | " | | |
| " " | 31st | " | Our artillery cut some hostile wire, a patrol of our repelled no hostile working parties out, so our 14 guns did not fire. | |

# WAR DIARY / INTELLIGENCE SUMMARY

Army Form C. 2118.

No. 102 M.G. Coy.

VOL. 8 1v 5

| Place | Date | Hour | Summary of Events and Information | Remarks and references to Appendices |
|---|---|---|---|---|
| ARMENTIERES | 1/9/16 | | Day and night quiet. M Gunn fires throughout the night. | |
| " | 20/9/16 | 10a.m. | Enemy shelled our front line. No 6329 L/cpl. W. Lea killed by a shell in front line. Will Trainer his L/cpl gunner. | |
| " | 29/9/16 | | Day fairly quiet. Hostile howitzer shelled frequently. Our artillery fired and hit cutting was carried out. Finch No 6710 L.a cpl died such damage to wire. Our M.G's searched WEZ MACQUART & Station, Distillery & gaps in the enemy's wire during the night | |
| " | 30/9/16 | 11.30 a.m. 1.30 | Enemy shelled our front line. Enemy shelled support line. Our artillery retaliated, air craft & enemy replied. No casualties. Our artillery fired. by knife artillery. Enemy reply poor. Slight damage in ARMENTIERES. By knife artillery done by poor shells. | |
| " | | 5.30 pm | Fairly severe retaliation bombarded. Little damage. Distillery and road. During the night our M.Gs searched station. bombarding system. | |
| " | 1/10/16 | | Early fairly quiet. Our artillery carried out wire cutting. Good results were obtained. The gap will repost when M.G. and Lewis gun fire. | |
| " | 2/10/16 | | Enemy artillery shelled ARMENTIERES Station with about 20 H.E. + 2 c.m. shells also the Railway to the E of it. Found 1 rd blind. The Enemy Field Artillery on their wire, were also seen digging WNW KW N of. | |

D.C. No. 102 M.G. Coy

# WAR DIARY
## INTELLIGENCE SUMMARY
*(Erase heading not required.)*

Army Form C. 2118.

102 M.G. Coy. VOL. 5.

| Place | Date | Hour | Summary of Events and Information | Remarks and references to Appendices |
|---|---|---|---|---|
| ARMENTIERES | 6/9/16 | 11 a.m. | Our artillery strafed a certain front and made several hits on the target at that point. | |
| | | 5 p.m. | Our artillery and T.M.B. carried out a combined scheme. Our M.G.s strafed the Distillery, Station, Hotel and the road joining them, also the wire in the gate during the night. Enemy shelled the railway at ARMENTIERES with about 20 4/7 m.m shells. | |
| | 7/9/16 | 1.45 a.m. | Our hostile aeroplane flew over ARMENTIERES. Our M.G. fired during the night. The day was quiet. | |
| | 8/9/16 | | Our artillery were active during the day firing on enemy's wire with good effect. | |
| | | 11.30 a.m. | Our Lytic's Guns fired, carrying out wire cutting. The shells fell well into the wire and did considerable damage, leaving gap in. Our M.G.s were very active throughout the night, strafing the enemy's wire and also the roads. | |
| | 9/9/16 | 6.45 a.m. | Hostile working party observed, fired on by our howitzers. The day fairly quiet, our artillery firing occasionally. | |
| | | 7.15 p.m. | Fired at any aeroplade flying over our lines. As they faded into green VERY light. | |
| | | | Our M.G. continued to search the gaps in enemy wire [illegible] the night. | 10 [illegible] Capt. |

O.C. No. 102 M.G. Co.

# WAR DIARY of INTELLIGENCE SUMMARY

No. 102 M.G. Coy. VOL 5.

Army Form C. 2118.

| Place | Date | Hour | Summary of Events and Information | Remarks and references to Appendices |
|---|---|---|---|---|
| ARMENTIERES | 10/9/16 | | Our artillery carried out wire cutting during the day. Otherwise the day passed quiet. Our M.G. and Lewis guns therefore the gaps in the enemy's wire throughout the night. One officer joined the Coy to replace ——— | |
| " | 11/9/16 | | During the day, hostile artillery fire on our support line. Our artillery and Trench Mortars retaliated with good effect. Patrols went out during the night, and observed working parties, who were fired on by own Lewis guns on the return of the patrols. Our M.Gs continued to search the gaps in the enemy's wire during the night. | |
| " | 12/9/16 | | Day passed quiet. M.Gs searched gaps in enemy's wire during the night. | |
| " | 13/9/16 | | Our artillery shewed a sustained O.P. A patrol went out and on their return that enemy were extremely quiet. Our M.G's were very active on enemy's wire during the night. | |
| " | 14/9/16 | 11pm | Large fire broke out in enemy's lines S of Railway, it extended for 700 yds and burnt for 45 mins. Enemy shelled our Subsidiary line about 150 rounds were fired from 4" m.m. 10.5.c.m. & 15.0 cm guns. Damage done to our support line. | |
| " | 15/9/16 | | The usual wire cutting operations were carried out by Artillery and Trench Mortars during the day. Leaving gaps in enemy's wire for M.Gs and Lewis guns were very active, leaving gaps in enemy's wire throughout night. | |

# WAR DIARY
## INTELLIGENCE SUMMARY

Army Form C. 2118.

No. 102 M.G. Coy. VOL. 5

| Place | Date | Hour | Summary of Events and Information | Remarks and references to Appendices |
|---|---|---|---|---|
| ARMENTIERES | 16/9/16 | 11.20 a.m. | Our artillery fired on a working party. They also fired on the Distillery Manager's House, and started to clear the wire cutting. | |
| | " | 1.30 a.m. | A patrol went out at 1.30 a.m. and found a wiring party at work. Our Lewis Guns opened fire on the party, when the patrol returned. Then Lewis Gun was carried out by our M.G's during the night. | |
| | " | | The usual teasing of gaps in the enemy's wire was carried out by our M.G's during the night. | |
| | 17/9/16 | 10 a.m. to 11.30 a.m. | Enemy fired 25 shells into the front and support trenches, N. of Rue-du-Bois Salient, wounding one man. | |
| | | | During the afternoon, enemy bombarded the Rue-du-Bois Salient lightly with artillery, minenwerfers, and rifle grenades. Slight damage was done. | |
| | " | 7 p.m. | Enemy fired several trench mortars, doing some damage. Rifle fire throughout the night. Our M.G's and Lewis guns were very active. | |
| | 18/9/16 | | During the morning our snipers were very active. A suspected M.G. Emplacement has been shelled by our Artillery. More rifle fire than usual was heard during the night. The enemy again shelled the Rue-Du-Bois Salient and support line with 5.9 c.m. and Trench Mortars and rifle grenades. Some damage was done to the trenches. | |
| | 19/9/16 | | Day was fairly quiet. Artillery carried out wire cutting during the night. I directed the wire cutting in the night. | |

**Army Form C. 2118.**

# WAR DIARY
## or
## INTELLIGENCE SUMMARY
*(Erase heading not required.)*

**No. 102 M.G. Coy.  VOL. 5**

| Place | Date | Hour | Summary of Events and Information | Remarks and references to Appendices |
|---|---|---|---|---|
| ARMENTIERES | 20/9/16 | 10.30pm | Our artillery and trench mortars carried out wire cutting and also fired on enemy's O.P's. A patrol went out to examine the wire. They found the front wire cut. Our M.G's continued to search enemy's wire during the night. | |
| " | 21/9/16 | | At 4.45am and 9.0am trench mortars were seen from enemy front line. They were seen working and were dispersed by our artillery fire. Enemy very quiet during last 24 hours. | |
| " | 22/9/16 | | In retaliation for our early morning bombardment — rifle & M.G. fire grenades and light minenwerfer were fired into the RUE-DU-BOIS salient. No damage was done. Our artillery were active during the day wire cutting. M.G's searched the gaps during the night. | |
| " | 23/9/16 | | Our artillery fired effectively on LARGE FARM, ESTAMINET de la BARRIERE, also on the DISTILLERY. | |
| | | 4pm | Our heavy trench mortars fired 8 rounds. The first burst in the communication trench, the second in the air over the enemy's support trench. | |
| | | 10.30pm | Standing patrols were out from both sectors, but did not encounter any hostile patrols or working parties. Later, the enemy was observed repairing his parapet. The artillery were informed and dispersed the party. Our Lewis Guns also fired on the gaps. Our M.G's continued to search the enemy wire, also gaps throughout the night. | |

# WAR DIARY
## INTELLIGENCE SUMMARY

**Army Form C. 2118.**

No. 102 M.G. Coy. VOL. 5

| Place | Date | Hour | Summary of Events and Information | Remarks and references to Appendices |
|---|---|---|---|---|
| ARMENTIERES | 24/4/16 | | During the day our trench mortars cut wire doing considerable damage. The artillery fired on the ESTAMINET de la BARRIERE, TOMBLLHOUSE, VEZ MACQUART, also the index N.E. of it. 12 rounds into the enemy's trenches completely silencing the Stokes guns fired 12 rounds into the enemy's trenches completely silencing enemy rifle grenade fire. Enemy artillery was very quiet during the day but their M.G.'s were very active during the night. Smoke was seen rising from the enemy trenches. | |
| " | " | 11:30am | A hostile aeroplane coming from the East, circled & turned in our wire opposite PARK ROW AVENUE. | |
| " | " | | Our M.G.'s were very active during the night. Playing on the gaps in the enemy's wire. | |
| " | " | 5:40 pm | During the day our artillery carried out wire cutting. Hostile artillery fired shrapnel & HE into ARMENTIERES & the gap in our trench on the big wood. Krupp guns were firing throughout the day on the enemy wire. | |
| " | 25/4/16 | 6:15 pm | Trench Mortars cut wire during the day. Smoke was observed in the enemy trenches about 6am. | |
| " | " | | The enemy shelled ARMENTIERES. No our area. Our artillery retaliated on PRESMESQUE. | |
| " | " | 12:30 pm | Enemy fired 12 rifle grenades into the RUE-DU-BOIS salient | |

W.J. Napier Capt.
O.C. No. 102 M.G. Coy

# WAR DIARY
## INTELLIGENCE SUMMARY

(Erase heading not required.) of No. 102 M.G. Coy.  **VOL 5.**

Army Form C. 2118.

| Place | Date | Hour | Summary of Events and Information | Remarks and references to Appendices |
|---|---|---|---|---|
| ARMENTIÈRES. | 27.9.16 | 3.45 p.m. | Wire was cut by medium French Mortars under cover of the artillery firing on TOWELL HORSE, LARGE FARM, ESTAMINET-de-la-BARRIÈRE, & WEZ MACQUART. | |
| " | " | 3.50pm | The enemy T.M's fired on MANAGER'S HOUSE, the shot fell near the enemy front line. | |
| " | " | 6pm | Enemy shelled ARMENTIÈRES and CHAPELLE D'ARMENTIÈRES | |
| " | " | 7.30pm | Enemy shelled the LILLE ROAD. During the night our M.G's traversed the gaps in the enemy's wire. | |
| " | 28/9/16 | | Our artillery and T.M's carried out wire cutting during the day. During the afternoon the enemy shelled ARMENTIÈRES. Our M.G's fired throughout the night, searching the gaps in the enemy's wire. | |
| " | 29/9/16 | | Our artillery carried out wire cutting during the day with success. Standing patrols were put out during the night, no wire return on M.G's fired on the enemy wire. | |
| " | 30/9/16 | 10pm | The 23rd N.F. carried out a raid in the enemy's trenches. They captured 1 wounded man and brought in the dead body of a Lieut of Infantry. Entered the German lines. They found them un-occupied. Our M.G's fired during the night on the return of the raiding parties. | |

O.S.H.W.R. Capt.
O.C. No. 102 M.G. Coy.

**Army Form C. 2118.**

**WAR DIARY**
or
INTELLIGENCE SUMMARY

(Erase heading not required.) of 102. Machine Gun Coy. Vol 6

| Place | Date | Hour | Summary of Events and Information | Remarks and references to Appendices |
|---|---|---|---|---|
| ARMENTIERES | 1/10/16 | 6am | Working parties were heard on the enemy's parapet and were fired on by our snipers. | |
| | | 11am | Enemy fired 8 rounds 10.5 and 15 c.m. on trench 62 and DEAD COW FARM. | |
| | | 2pm | 5 rounds were fired into the support line by DEAD COW FARM. | |
| | | 2.30 pm | 4 rounds were fired into RUE-DU-BOIS salient. | |
| | | | During the afternoon, he shelled ARMENTIERES, N of our area. | |
| | | 10pm | Stores were heard in enemy's line near the LILLE RD. Our M.G's continued to fire through the night, searching gaps in the enemy's wire. | |
| | 2/10/16 | | The day passed quiet. Stokes guns fired frequently. Enemy shelled ARMENTIERES in the afternoon. Our M.G's fired throughout the night on the enemy's wire. | |
| | 3/10/16 | | Enemy were quiet during the day. Our artillery and T.M's carried out wire cutting during the afternoon. | |
| | | 7.30pm | Working parties were fired on by our artillery. Our M.G's were active during the night, to prevent enemy repairing his wire. | |

J Rutherford 2nd Lt for Capt
O.C. No. 102 M.G. Coy

Army Form C. 2118.

# WAR DIARY
or
## INTELLIGENCE SUMMARY

(Erase heading not required.) of No 102. Machine Gun Company

| Place | Date | Hour | Summary of Events and Information | Remarks and references to Appendices |
|---|---|---|---|---|
| ARMENTIERES | 4/10/16 | 2-45 pm | Our medium T.M's cut wire, while the artillery fired on LARGE FARM, SNIPER'S HOUSE, and buildings from ESTAMINET-de-LA-BARRIERE to WEZ MACQUART. | |
| | | 3pm | The light T.M's fired 40 rounds and again at 4pm 10 rounds considerable damage being done. | |
| | | 4pm | O.R. Graham wounded though sheltered by sniper. | |
| | | 1.30am | A working party was spotted on the enemy's wire. They were dispersed by our Vickers and Lewis guns. | |
| | | 10.30 to 11.15 | Enemy bombarded ARMENTIERES, N. of our area, setting fire to 2 buildings. Our artillery retaliated. M.G's were very busy during the night. | |
| | 5/10/16 | 2.30pm | The enemy fired 10 rifle-grenades into CHARDS FARM. and MINERS LANE doing slight damage. Trench mortars were very quiet during the day. | |
| | | 4.30pm | Enemy artillery and our M.G's were [    ] firing throughout the night. Our artillery were very active and our M.G's were [    ] firing throughout the night. | |
| | 6/10/16 | 3-10pm | The medium T.M's cut wire. The covering artillery fired on LARGE FARM, SNIPER'S HOUSE, BREWERY, and buildings from ESTAMINET-DE-LA-BARRIERE and WEZ MACQUART. Enemy were quiet during the day. Our M.G's fired on the enemy wire throughout the night. | |

J Rutherford Lieut for

Army Form C. 2118.

# WAR DIARY or INTELLIGENCE SUMMARY

(Erase heading not required.) of No. 102. Machine Gun Company.

Instructions regarding War Diaries and Intelligence Summaries are contained in F. S. Regs., Part II. and the Staff Manual respectively. Title Pages will be prepared in manuscript.

| Place | Date | Hour | Summary of Events and Information | Remarks and references to Appendices |
|---|---|---|---|---|
| ARMENTIERES | 7/10 | 3.30 pm | Our artillery cut wire. The Trench Mortars also fired, doing considerable damage. The enemy side continued to throw bombs into their own wire during the night. | |
| | | 4pm | Without apparent reason 6 shells smaller than 77 m.m. during the day. The enemy fired 30. 77 m.m. shells on to our trench, doing no damage. | |
| | | 5pm | Enemy fired 30. 77 m.m. shells on to our trench, doing no damage. They also fired 10 heavy minenwerfer and 30 pineapples, doing no damage. Our M.Gs continued to fire on gaps in enemy wire throughout the night. | |
| | 8/10/16 | | The artillery made direct hits on an supposed enemy T.M. emplacement. The enemy were generally quiet. Stokes gun fired 40 rounds, doing considerable damage. Our M.Gs fired continually during the night. | |
| | 9/10/16 | 3.20pm | Enemy fired 5 minenwerfer on to our trench and again at 4.30pm | |
| | | 3.25pm | They fired 14 into the same place. Our Stokes gun retaliated. The night however was very quiet. | |
| | 10/10/16 | 4pm | Our heavy T.Ms considerably damaged the wire. At the same time the enemy fired 4 rounds at GERMAN HOUSE. Covering artillery fired at the DISTILLERY and the supports. The enemy continued to throw bombs in his own wire. During the night our M.Gs were very active. | |

Rutherford ?/Lt/Capt

O.C. 102 m.G. Coy

# WAR DIARY or INTELLIGENCE SUMMARY

Army Form C. 2118.

(Erase heading not required.) of No: 152 Machine Gun Coy

| Place | Date | Hour | Summary of Events and Information | Remarks and references to Appendices |
|---|---|---|---|---|
| ARMENTIERES | 11/10/16 | 9 a.m. 4.45 p.m. | Enemy fired 27 10.5 c.m. shells doing very little damage. They fired 30 10.5 c.m. shells, 40 minenwerfers, and 10. 4.4 m.m. shells over a French T.M. allowed to be firing. The enemy bombarded CHARD'S FARM with minenwerfers. Our artillery retaliated and apparently made a direct hit as smoke was seen to rise and minenwerfer fire ceased. Our M.G. continued to search the gaps in the wire throughout the night. | |
| " | 12/10/16 | 4.30 p.m. | A raid was carried out by the 1st T.I. They entered the enemy's trenches and remained for 16 minutes during which time they bombed 12 dugouts and inflicted between 30 and 40 casualties on the enemy. 4 prisoners were taken. Here attempted to retake and were killed. Our artillery and T.M. bombarded most effective The enemy still continue to throw bombs in to own wire. During the raid, the enemy retaliated with heavy minenwerfers on CHARD'S FARM, MINER'S LANE and the C.O.C. Dugout. MINER'S LANE was completely knocked in and 1 officer and 3 men were killed, 8 men wounded. 4.4 m.m. and lights shells were fired over the whole front without doing any damage. | |

Hillinger 2/Lt for Capt
OC. 152 M.G. Coy

# WAR DIARY
## or
## INTELLIGENCE SUMMARY

Army Form C. 2118.

(Erase heading not required) No 162 M.G. Coy

| Place | Date | Hour | Summary of Events and Information | Remarks and references to Appendices |
|---|---|---|---|---|
| ARMENTIERES | 13/10/16 | | The day passed very quiet. Our artillery carried out some wire cutting. Enemy continued to throw bombs into his own trenches throughout the night. Our M.Gs were very busy searching the gaps during the night. | |
| " | 14/10/16 | | Our snipers were very active during the day. Enemy artillery quiet. Their M.Gs were very quiet during the day but there was a great deal of M.G. and rifle fire spray the night. Our M.Gs carried out their usual firing throughout the night. | |
| " | 15/10/16 | 0.36/m | Our This cut wire. The evening artillery fire on LA HOUSSOIE, THE DISTILLERY, & MANAGER'S HOUSE. Enemy continually used a searchlight in the neighbourhood of WEZ MACQUART during the night. M.G. were usually active. | |
| " | 16/10/16 | | The enemy retaliated to our fire with rifle grenades, minenwerfer, and 77 MM shells, over the whole front from RUE-DU-BOIS salient to PARK AVENUE. Considerable damage was done in the salient by these were no casualties. Night passed fairly quiet. | |

J. Rutherford Capt
O.C. 162 M.G. Coy

# WAR DIARY
## INTELLIGENCE SUMMARY

Of No: 162. M. G. Coy.

Army Form C. 2118.

| Place | Date | Hour | Summary of Events and Information | Remarks and references to Appendices |
|---|---|---|---|---|
| ARMENTIERES | 17/10/16 | 4.45pm | The enemy anti-aircraft guns made a direct hit on one of our aeroplanes flying over the enemy's lines. The aeroplane came down in pieces, one of the occupants was observed to fall out as the aeroplane was falling. Enemy fired 4 10c.m. shells into the SHORT line. He also fired 8 4.7c.m. shells. These fell short in NO MAN'S LAND. He similarly in SALOP AVENUE. Aircraft was very active throughout the day on both sides. | |
| | 18/10/16 | 6.30 am | The artillery carried out a bombardment of GRAND MARIAS, PETIT MARIAS, and CHATEAU D'HANCARDY. | |
| | | 2.8pm | The Stokes gun bombarded GERMAN HOUSE, doing considerable damage. This was in retaliation to hostile T.M. fire. A wiring party was disturbed by our Lewis guns. The enemy searchlight was again very active in the neighbourhood of MEZ MACQUART. The enemy shelled the CHORD LINE, one dropping short in NO MAN'S LAND. They fired bombs from T.M. shells into the RUE du-BOIS behind. No damage was done. A hostile aeroplane flew over our lines, but was driven back by our A.A. guns. He fired 12 anti-aircraft guns in the front of the lights. | |

Ruston Hubart Lt.
O.C. 162 M.G. Coy.

# WAR DIARY or INTELLIGENCE SUMMARY

No 102 Machine Gun Coy.

Army Form C. 2118.

| Place | Date | Hour | Summary of Events and Information | Remarks and references to Appendices |
|---|---|---|---|---|
| ARMENTIERES | 19/10/16 | 11.45 a.m. | The medium T.M's cut wire. Two lanes were practically cut through. The covering artillery fired on the houses between LARGE FARM & HEZ MACQUART. The enemy retaliated throwing bombs into his wire, and to sweep NO MANS LAND, with very poor M.G. fire. Flarelights were used during the night, on behind HEZ MACQUART. Our M.G's were very active on the gaps in the enemy's wire throughout the night. | |
| | 20/10/16 | 4.30 a.m. | 10 15cm shells fell into the CHORD LINE and again at 2.45 p.m. 4 4.10.5 shells. O duty outward badly damaged. Enemy flarelights were very active during the night. M.G's were firing the whole of this night. | |
| | | 1.30 p.m. | Our machine gun's were very active throughout the day. Enemy guns & M.G's endeavouring on to support theirs and again at opened. There fire was silenced by our artillery. Also fire by supporting batties. Some divisions of our artillery also fired by night. | |
| | 22/10/16 | 6.30 p.m. | During the day. This carried out wire cutting. A raid was carried out by the 3rd M.G. They found the enemy waiting for them. German wounded and bombs were thrown into the German trenches. The party returned without any casualty. 1 officer and one man wounded. Wright 4th for battle. One man missing. Battery Hercules. The men is missing. O.C. 102 M.G. Coy. | |

# WAR DIARY or INTELLIGENCE SUMMARY

Army Form C. 2118.

(Erase heading not required.)

| Place | Date | Hour | Summary of Events and Information | Remarks and references to Appendices |
|---|---|---|---|---|
| Armentières | 22/10/16 | Last night | During the raid enemy M.G's were very active along the line. In retaliation the enemy fired Light Minenwerfer, most of which were blind, into CHARDS FARM, doing little damage. | |
| " | 23/10/16 | | A detail of 4 men under of S. Yates, 125416 went out and proceeded to ford the Douvés River. The ground was very marshy. Sounds of enemy working party were heard from the Enemy lines. Lewis guns were also opened on all party on sight of his patrol. Men were very active by night. | |
| " | 24/10/16 | | In retaliation to the shelling of Brown, the enemy retaliated with heavy and light Tello on PARK ROW AVENUE. | |
| | | 2.15 p.m. | Enemy again shelled BURNT FARM. During the afternoon he shelled his support lines behind WILTON AVENUE. The bombardment was very heavy. | |
| | 25/10/16 | from 2-3 p.m. to 3.30 p.m. | The artillery and Trench mortars carried out combined scheme. The medium did some damage to the wire. | |
| | | 3.45 p.m. | Artillery fired on the supporting line SNIPER'S HOUSE. Enemy began trench bombs throughout the night. | |

Rutherford Lt/Col
O.C. No. 102 M.G. Coy.

# WAR DIARY or INTELLIGENCE SUMMARY

Army Form C. 2118.

(Erase heading not required) *No 10 2 M. G. Coy*

| Place | Date | Hour | Summary of Events and Information | Remarks and references to Appendices |
|---|---|---|---|---|
| ARMENTIERES | 26/10/16 | 0.45 am. | The enemy fired 5. 77mm on the Suffolk line between SALOP AV. and RUE du BOIS. Shrapnel burst over WINE AVENUE & QUEEN ST; one shell burst in the trench. | |
| " | " | 9.30 am | Enemy retaliated to our fire with 25. 77mm and 12 lineaflies into the further, between WILLOW WALK and PARK ROW. He also fired Minenwerfer which fell short. | |
| " | " | 11.15 pm | He fired again 3. 77mm into our Suffolk line between SALOP AV. Our Vm Gs were very active during the night. | |
| " | 27/10/16 | | Enemy retaliated to our short with 8 heavy minenwerfer H fell in CHARDS FARM, doing no damage. Enemy rifle & m.g fire was very quiet during the night but our guns continued towards the gaps in the wire. | |
| " | 28/10/16 | | Enemy artillery was very active throughout the day. Shrapnel burst over SALOP AV, RUE-du-BOIS, R/the SWITCH LINE & on the railway. Our Stokes guns retaliated | |

Rutherford 2/Lt M C Capt
OC 102 M G Coy

**Army Form C. 2118.**

# WAR DIARY or INTELLIGENCE SUMMARY

(Erase heading not required.) of No. 102. M. G. Coy

| Place | Date | Hour | Summary of Events and Information | Remarks and references to Appendices |
|---|---|---|---|---|
| ARMENTIERES | 28/10/16 (cont) | | Remainder of the day fairly quiet. Our Artillery slightly wounded in hand. Our M.G. fired during the night. | |
| " | 29/10/16 | | Artillery and T.M.s carried out wire cutting around the day. Enemy retaliated, doing damage to LEITH WALK. Our M.G.s were again very active throughout the night. | |
| " | 30/10/16 | | Sgt C.A.A. Stouge joined from Base Depot. Wire cutting was carried out by heavy T.M.s Enemy were very quiet. The T.M.s continued to throw bombs into his own wire. M.G. carried out the usual harassing during the night. | |
| " | 31/10/16 | | Company relieved with few casualties. The usual wire cutting was carried out during the day by artillery and T.M.s and M.G.s fired to keep the gaps open during the night. | Hutchinson Lieut. Lr. O.C. 102. M.G. Coy. 06.16.2. Coy |

Army Form C. 2118.

# WAR DIARY
or
## INTELLIGENCE SUMMARY
(Erase heading not required.)

of No 102. M. G. Coy.    Vol VIII

Vol 7

| Place | Date | Hour | Summary of Events and Information | Remarks and references to Appendices |
|---|---|---|---|---|
| ARMENTIERES | 1/11/16 | | Lieut Sturge relieved of heatsome. During the firing of 3 guns, buffer cups of each broke in the same place. The guns continued to harass the enemy's wire throughout the night. | |
| " | 2/11/16 | | Our guns co-operated in the left group scheme firing on communication trenches. Cpl Holohan wounded while on sentry about 11.55pm. 9.25 left arm. Guns carried out usual nightly harassing of enemy's wire. | |
| " | 3/11/16 | | At night. 3 guns were taken from Coy H.Q. to 1, 2 and 3 positions. The usual operations were carried out. | |
| " | 4/11/16 | | The artillery carried out wire cutting during the day. Our teams continued to strengthen their emplacements. The guns were busy during the night keeping gaps in the enemy's wire open. | |
| " | 5/11/16 | | The day passed quietly, usual artillery work being carried out. Our guns continued to fire during the night on the ridge. | Ruttonjel for Capt O.C. 102 M.G. Coy |

# WAR DIARY or INTELLIGENCE SUMMARY

(Erase heading not required.) of No 102. M. G. Coy

Army Form C. 2118.

| Place | Date | Hour | Summary of Events and Information | Remarks and references to Appendices |
|---|---|---|---|---|
| ARMENTIERES. | 6/1/16 | 5:35pm | During the afternoon some artillery bombardment heavily. Enemy retaliated. L/Cpl Bealf was wounded in the A.P.P. M&G fire during the night. | |
| | 7/1/16 | | A raid was carried out by the N.F. Lieut Armitage wounded in the shoulder. | |
| | 8/1/16 | | A raid was carried out by the 23rd N.F. after 5 minutes bombardment. The party entered the enemy trenches. Trenches were found empty but traces of their dead were found in dug outs. | |
| | 9/1/16 | | The enemy were very active throughout the day and entered our trench to his own front line. Our guns fired on the wire by night. | |
| | 10/1/16 | | Enemy artillery were very active during the day. Gun teams continued to work on dugouts and gun emplacements. Cpl Mathers admitted to hospital. | |
| | 11/1/16 | | Lieut S.A. Crofton posted to the Company as 2nd/c vice Capt. J.P. Gott transferred to take command of 184 M.G. Coy. | |
| | 12/1/16 | | Our teams continued to strengthen their dug outs. Guns continued to fire by night. | |

Matthews Lt. p/c a/Lt.
O.C. 102. M.G. Coy.

**Army Form C. 2118.**

# WAR DIARY
## or
## INTELLIGENCE SUMMARY

(Erase heading not required.) of No: 102 M.G. Coy

Instructions regarding War Diaries and Intelligence Summaries are contained in F.S. Regs., Part II. and the Staff Manual respectively. Title Pages will be prepared in manuscript.

| Place | Date | Hour | Summary of Events and Information | Remarks and references to Appendices |
|---|---|---|---|---|
| Ammuntiere | 13/1/16 | | Lieut Owen joined the Company. The Bentley, Walkers and Hack returned to the Bde. Guns fired throughout the night. | |
| " | 14/1/16 | | Draft of 1 L/Naller and 1 Gunner joined from Base Depot. Lieut Owen relieved Lieut Newton. Gun teams continued to strengthen dug out gits during the day. The guns were very active throughout the night firing on the enemy's wire. | |
| " | 15/1/16 | | Capt Cadden and Laurell returned to oversee when artillery retaliated. Gun from the Hafuls team received during the day. Our artillery retaliated. Enemy artillery was very active during the afternoon. Our artillery was also very active during the day. Aircraft was also very active during the day. Our M.G.s fired as usual by night on paths to the enemy's wire. One stretcher returned from hospital. | |
| " | 16/1/16 | 4 pm. | In cooperation with artillery and Trench Mortar Batteries Machine Gun fire was directed on WEZ MACQUART ROAD (I.16,a,5,3 – I.23,a,7,0.) and enemy communication trenches I.22,4,0,8 – I.22,b,64 and I.21,a,24 – I.27 a 64 | Shot 30 N W Bdl 6c. |
| " | 17/1/16 | 8½ pm 12 m.n. | Guns fired on enemy communication trenches our superior dumps | |

Rutherford. Lt
O.C. 102 M.G. Coy

# WAR DIARY or INTELLIGENCE SUMMARY

of 102 M.G. Coy

| Place | Date | Hour | Summary of Events and Information | Remarks and references to Appendices |
|---|---|---|---|---|
| ARMENTIERES | 17/11/16 | 3 am | Gun L4475 hit by a bullet, which jammed the barrel casing. Hole patched with Plasticine. | |
| | | 9 am | Gun L4475 relieved, and sent to Armoures for repair. | |
| | 18/11/16 | | Enemy M.G. emplacement outpriced at I.22.a.3.8. Usual M.G. activity during the night. | |
| | | 9 am | Lieut. W.G.P. Dragby posted for one month's instruction to C.O. 21st N.F. Lieut. G. Bell posted for one month's instruction to C.O. 23rd N.F. Lieut. Graham 21st N.F. } attached to 102 M.G. Coy for one month's instruction in and Lieut. Wilmott 23rd N.F. } the duties of M.G. Section officer. 2/Lt Graham attached to Lieut OWEN, 2nd Wilmott to Lieut NEWSOME.  During night guns fired on enemy dumps and communication trenches. | |
| | 20/11/16 | | Machine Gun Emplacement (Enemy) outposts at I.16.d.5,7. Usual programme of firing carried out. | |
| | 21/11/16 | 2.30 am | Pte NICHOLS, whilst on duty with gun, received a bullet wound in the jaw. Pte Nicholas admitted to 2nd Aus C.C.S. and a truck of strength of Coy. | |
| | 23/11/16 | 4 am | Gun limber, damaged by carrying heavy R.E. material sent to Mobile Workshop for repair. Pte King F. wounded in chest by bullet. | |

Witherspoon Lieut for

# WAR DIARY or INTELLIGENCE SUMMARY

Army Form C. 2118.

| Place | Date | Hour | Summary of Events and Information | Remarks and references to Appendices |
|---|---|---|---|---|
| ARMENTIERES | 23/4/16 contd. | 8.11 pm | A Raiding Party of 21st NF (2nd Tyneside Scottish) entered enemy trench at I.21.c.15.00. Some dead Germans were seen and there felts and there forks were brought back. A party from the Bn. on our right front stood was firing upon and did not succeed in entering the enemy's trench. Casualties slight. Trench Mortars (medium) cut wire at I.21.c.60.14, I.21.c.22.00 and I.16.d.25.30. During night M.G. fire and Lewis Gun fire were brought to bear on these gaps to prevent enemy repairing them. An O.P. was reported at I.26.d.10.15, when there is a turn in a line with a ladder leading up to it. A hostile Machine Gun which open during the bombardment was silenced by our artillery. | |
| | 24/4/16 | | Lieut F.M. DIXON, 63rd Northumbrian Div Cyclist Corps reported for duty with the Bn. Hostile Machine Guns not active during the night. Very lights were fired from support lines opposite RUE du BOIS Salier. A barrier has been erected in front of the BARRIER at I.22.b.60.25 M.G. fire brought to bear on gaps in wire, suspend dumps, and communication trenches. | |
| | 25/4/16 | | Gun L 3709 sent to Ordnance Workshop for repair — one rifle plate injured. Corporal Bough returned from 35th G.H.Q. School Mitaulleur, OSTIERS | |

Rutherford Lieut for

# WAR DIARY
## or
## INTELLIGENCE SUMMARY.
(Erase heading not required.) of 102 M.G. Coy.

Army Form C. 2118.

| Place | Date | Hour | Summary of Events and Information | Remarks and references to Appendices |
|---|---|---|---|---|
| ARMENTIERES. | 23/11/16 6 p.m. | | A hostile M.G. emplacement is suspected at T 32 c 1590, when there is a bon loop hole low down on parapet. A hostile Gun is reported to fire from her at night. | |
| | 26/11/16 | | Private Sedgwick E transferred to 102 M.G. Coy, from 103 M.G. Coy. Binoculars Zeiss this. loté in tray of house at I 26 b 65,35. There was increased machine gun fire and rifle fire at 'stand to'. Enemy continues to throw bombs into his wire. Pte Ronald wounded in head by a bullet. | |
| | 27/11/16 | | Hostile Machine Guns continue more active. Several bullets struck the wall of houses at RUE POST. Lieut DIXON relieves Lieut STURGE. | |
| | 28/11/16 | | Lieut C.H.P. STURGE of Lewis/Capt Palmer R, Pte Higley and Pte HERMAN left Coy. to attend 36th Course at G.H.Q. Machine Gun School CAMIERS. Usual M.G. Activity during night. | |
| | 29/11/16 | 1 p.m. 1.45 p.m. | Active ed by T.M.B. (Medium) I 21 b 50 24, I 21 b 6918 and I 21 D 33 23. Arty/right M.G. fire was directed on gaps in wire, and on enemy communication trenches round LAHOUSSOIE. | |

T2134. Wt. W708—776. 500000. 4/15. Sir J. C. & S.

[signature] Lieut for

Fol 9.

Army Form C. 2118.

# WAR DIARY
## or
## INTELLIGENCE SUMMARY.
(Erase heading not required.)

of 102 F.A. Ly. Coy

| Place | Date | Hour | Summary of Events and Information | Remarks and references to Appendices |
|---|---|---|---|---|
| ARMENTIERES. | 29/11/16 | | Ptes Sharp W. and Gilbert J.W. returned to Base under age. | |
| | 30/11/16 | | Sgt Rowe and Pte Rowles Elliott (7th strength Nov) both admitted to 2 Aus. C.C.S. Lieut M.B. Chapple (Spotted Horse) joined the Coy for duty, and took over duties of Transport Officer. Day quiet on our front, Considerable artillery activity on left flank. | |

J Rutherford Lt
FC 102 F.A. LyCy

Vol 8

War Diary
Dec 1916

102 M G Coy

Army Form C. 2118.

# WAR DIARY
## or
## INTELLIGENCE SUMMARY.
(Erase heading not required.)

of 102 M.G. Coy.

Instructions regarding War Diaries and Intelligence Summaries are contained in F.S. Regs., Part II. and the Staff Manual respectively. Title pages will be prepared in manuscript.

| Place | Date | Hour | Summary of Events and Information | Remarks and references to Appendices |
|---|---|---|---|---|
| ARMENTIERES. | 1-12-16 | | During night Machine Gun fire was directed upon gaps in enemy wire from I.22.a.40.70 to I.21.b.30.15 and at I.21.c.62.15. Their communication trenches and tracks round the brickstacks in HOUSSOYE were freely sprinkled during night also. | |
| | 2-12-16 | | Day very quiet — M.G's active as usual | |
| | 3-12-16 | | Enemy wire cut in enemy wire by M.T.M. Batteries at I.26.c.84.p.3, I.22.a.29.56 I.22.a.43.75, I.22.a.54.82. Machine Gun fire was directed on these gaps during the night to prevent the enemy executing repairs. 6000 rounds expended. | |
| | 4-12-16 | | More gaps were made in enemy's wire at I.32.c.09.90, I.31.a.44.50, I.21.b.68.18 I.21.b.80.75 and I. These gaps were kept open by fire from our machine guns | |
| | 5-12-16 | | Enemy on gaps continues during night. | |
| | 6-12-16 | | A strong patrol left our trenches at midnight 6th/7th/12 to discover enemy dispositions in his front line trenches, and disarm and report on failure and condition | |

Rutherford Lt for
O.C. 102 M.G. Coy.

Army Form C. 2118.

# WAR DIARY
# or
# INTELLIGENCE SUMMARY.
(Erase heading not required.) 1/102 M.G. Coy

| Place | Date | Hour | Summary of Events and Information | Remarks and references to Appendices |
|---|---|---|---|---|
| ARMENITIERES | 6.12.16 | | condition of the enemy's wire and trenches in rear of his front line trench. Six machine guns were laid beforehand on the DISTILLERY RD. These guns were to fire on any hostile searchlights that might be alive, while the patrol was out. The guns did not fire. After patrol returned the machine guns carried out their usual firing on gaps in enemy wire. | |
| | | 5 p.m. | A party of chiefly O.R. — N section in Reserve — were inoculated. | |
| | 7.12.16 | | Firing on gaps continued during the night. Day quiet. | |
| | 8.12.16 | | M.G. Acting as usual. — gaps kept open. | |
| | 9.12.16 | | Enemy shelled cross roads CHAPPELLE D'ARMENTIERES with H.E and SHRAPNEL — no material damage done. | |
| | 10.12.16 | | Day quiet — firing on gaps continued. | |
| | 11.12.16 | 1.10 a.m. | Two raiding parties entered enemy's line at I 22 a 14.44 and I 22 a 28.57. Enemy trenches were found to be in good repair, having concrete dug outs with iron doors. A hostile active M.G. near I 22 a 38.59 with emplacement was blown up with explosives. | |

J. Rutherford Lt for  
O.C. 102 M.G. Coy

**WAR DIARY**
or
**INTELLIGENCE SUMMARY**
(Erase heading not required.)  of 102 M.G. Coy

Army Form C. 2118.

| Place | Date | Hour | Summary of Events and Information | Remarks and references to Appendices |
|---|---|---|---|---|
| ARMENTIERES | 11-12-16 Contd. | 1.10 a.m. | An enemy dump was blown up with a Stokes shell. The German fuzes were obtained at of 18th BAVARIAN INFY REGT. Some equipment and rifles were brought back. Our gunners are known to have been killed. Our casualties slight. Apparently him red rockets trouble into his own lines was the S.O.S. signal. After raid was finished M.G.S. carried out their usual programme of firing on suspected dumps, on roads, and communication trenches round and near WEZ MACQUART and LA HOUSSOYE. 103rd M.G. Coy relieved us in the trenches. | |
| | 12-12-16 | 12 noon | The whole company moved back to Billets at LAUNDRY H.5.a. SECHE RUE. Coy H.Q. established at H.4.d.4.6 ERQUINGHEM. 103rd M.G. Coy transport took over our standing at H.9.a.21.; our transport moved to standing at LA BOUDRELLE. A party of 50 men bathed in divisional Baths. | Hutcheon Cpt OC 102 M.G. Coy |

**Army Form C. 2118.**

# WAR DIARY
## or
## INTELLIGENCE SUMMARY.
*(Erase heading not required.)*

Vol 9 of 102nd M. G. Coy

Instructions regarding War Diaries and Intelligence Summaries are contained in F. S. Regs., Part II. and the Staff Manual respectively. Title pages will be prepared in manuscript.

| Place | Date | Hour | Summary of Events and Information | Remarks and references to Appendices |
|---|---|---|---|---|
| ERQUINGHEM | 13/12/16 | 10 a.m. | Party of 100 men bathed. | |
| " | 14/12/16 | 2.30 to 4.30 p.m. | A party of 1 Officer and 30 men were detailed as a working party for road making and C.R.E. 34th Div. | |
| | | | Programme of Training submitted to Bde. H.Q. | |
| " | 15/12/16 | 7.45 a.m. to 12 noon | Working party 1 Off. 30 O.R. detailed for work under C.R.E. on Rifle Range. ERQUINGHEM | |
| " | 16/12/16 | | Party of 30 O.R. inoculated. 2Lieut G. BELL transferred to 2nd Army Central School, Auly. 2nd Army P/22-13 a/10-12-16 - under age. | |
| " | 16/12/16 | 12.30 p.m to 4.30 | Working Party 1 Off. 30 O.R. - Rifle Range. Sergt Rowe reported for duty from Moulsdal. Pte Highton sent to 2nd Army Central School as orderly for Lt Bell. Divisional Commander inspected billets. | |
| " | 17/12/16 | | Working Party 1 Off. 30 O.R. - Rifle Range. | |

Rutherford 2/Lt
O.C. 102 M.G. Coy

Army Form C. 2118.

# WAR DIARY
## or
## INTELLIGENCE SUMMARY.
(Erase heading not required.)

Instructions regarding War Diaries and Intelligence Summaries are contained in F. S. Regs., Part II. and the Staff Manual respectively. Title pages will be prepared in manuscript.

| Place | Date | Hour | Summary of Events and Information | Remarks and references to Appendices |
|---|---|---|---|---|
| ERQUINGHEM | 18/12/16 | 1 pm | Corps Commander inspected Billets. | |
| | | 7.30 to 4.30 | Working party ] Working party ] 1 Off 30 O.R. for work on Rifle Range. | |
| | 19/12/16 | 11 am | Brigade Commander inspected the Company. Two guns mounted for Anti-aircraft work at LAUNDRY 17.5.a | |
| | | 8 pm | H 4 d 5.6. Material drawn from R.E. Yard for making Latrines. | |
| | 20/12/16 | 12.30 to 4.30 | Working party 1 Off 30 O.R. - Rifle Range. | |
| | | 1 pm | Enemy shelled ERQUINGHEM H 4 d will 5.9 A.E. | |
| | | 6 pm | Xmas dinner for the Company. | |
| | 21/12/16 | 8 am to 4 pm | 16 O.R. including 1 N.C.O detailed for work at R.E. Yard ERQUINGHEM | |

Rutupos Bgn
O.C. 102/17 of Coy

T2134. Wt. W708—776. 500000. 4/15. Sir J. C. & S.

Army Form C. 2118.

# WAR DIARY
# or
# INTELLIGENCE SUMMARY.

(Erase heading not required.)

of 102 M.G. Coy

Instructions regarding War Diaries and Intelligence Summaries are contained in F. S. Regs., Part II. and the Staff Manual respectively. Title pages will be prepared in manuscript.

| Place | Date | Hour | Summary of Events and Information | Remarks and references to Appendices |
|---|---|---|---|---|
| ERQUINGHEM | 22-12-16 | 12 noon | The 34th Division paraded for inspection on the FORT ROMPU - ERQUINGHEM ROAD. by the C.in.C. Sir Douglas HAIG. | |
| | | 3pm | Ribbons were packed and preparations made for the company to take over trenches from 103rd M.G. Coy | |
| ERQUINGHEM | 23-12-16 | 10.15 am | 'A' section under Lieut C.A.D. STURGE moved off en route for trenches. There four Gun teams took over positions 1, 2, 3 & 4 in front line trench. 'B' and 'C' sections followed at 5 min intervals. Gun teams 5, 6, 7 & 8 took on positions 6, 7, 8, 9 in support line. Gun teams 9, 10, 11, 12 took up position 5 in support and 10, 11, 12 in subsidiary line. Gun teams 4, 6, 7, 8, 9 are under control and supervision of 2Lt R.F. OWEN. " 2, 3, 5 under control and supervision of 2Lt C.A.D. STURGE. " 1, 10, 11 under control and supervision of 2Lt T.H. DIXON. 10, 12 Gun is under the direct control of the 2nd in command Lt S.A. COWPER MC. Coy Head Quarters established at RUE MARLE. | |
| ARMENTIERES | 23-12-16 | 3 pm | | |
| | | 3.15 | Relief reported complete at 3.15 pm. | |

Ruttuth Lt ? 
O.C. 102 M.G. Coy

# WAR DIARY
## or
## INTELLIGENCE SUMMARY.
*(Erase heading not required.)*

Army Form C. 2118.

| Place | Date | Hour | Summary of Events and Information | Remarks and references to Appendices |
|---|---|---|---|---|
| ARMENTIERES | 24-12-16 | | With reference to the inspection on 22nd inst, the C in C congratulates all ranks on their smart turn out and excellent behaviour. He was particularly struck with the steadiness of the men in the ranks, the good marching and the effort the men made to show up well inspite of adverse climatic conditions. | |
| | | 6pm | Duplicate return of trench stores taken over sent to Bde H.Q. Machine Gun Mountings for Anti aircraft work have been installed at I.15.b.3.3 and I.15.c.5.15 on Lille Post Area. The usual sniping and harassing fire was maintained on enemy heads and trenches round and near WEZ MACQUART and LA HOUSSOYE | |
| " | 24-12-16 | 2pm | 2 Lieut H. BURKETT 20th N.F. reported for duty with the Coy. | |
| " | 25-12-16 | | Lieut C.H.A. STURGE worked to C.O. 20th N.F. for duty with Rail Battn. Lieut W.Q.P. DONAGHY relieved 2/L C.H.A. STURGE in the trenches. Pte. Higley R. (13665) afforded Lance Corporal (unpaid). Lance Corporal Higley takes place of No 3 Gun failure vice Corporal HUTCHINS. | |

Army Form C. 2118.

# WAR DIARY
## or
## INTELLIGENCE SUMMARY.
(Erase heading not required.)

of 102 M.G. Coy

Instructions regarding War Diaries and Intelligence Summaries are contained in F. S. Regs., Part II. and the Staff Manual respectively. Title pages will be prepared in manuscript.

| Place | Date | Hour | Summary of Events and Information | Remarks and references to Appendices |
|---|---|---|---|---|
| ARMENTIERES | 25-12-16 | — | The C-in-C sent his Xmas greetings to the troops in the field. Working in cooperation with the R.A., 102 Stokes Mortar Battery, who carried out shoots on enemy trenches at 1 a.m., 2 p.m. and 3.30 p.m. Machine Gun fire was brought to bear on WEZ MACQUART, DISTILLERY ROAD, LA BARRIERE and Communication trenches near LA HOUSSOYE. | |
| do | 26-12-16 | — | Corporal Hutchins proceeded to 9 H.12 Machine Gun School Camiers to attend course of Instruction. | |
| do | 27-12-16 | 2 a.m. | Nos 13, 14, 15, 16 Gun Teams ("B" Sec) relieved 1, 2, 3, 4 ("A" Section) No 15239 Pte Ballson wounded in head and shoulder by a pineapple about 5 a.m. | |
| do | 28-12-16 | | During the night we carried out usual scheme of harassing fire on enemy front line and will also indirect fire on enemy's communications around the DISTILLERY, LA HOUSSOIE, 3250 rounds fired | |

J.J. Moroni Lieutenant
P.6. 102 M.G. Coy

Army Form C. 2118.

# WAR DIARY
## or
## INTELLIGENCE SUMMARY of No 102. M.G. Coy.
(Erase heading not required.)

Instructions regarding War Diaries and Intelligence Summaries are contained in F. S. Regs., Part II. and the Staff Manual respectively. Title pages will be prepared in manuscript.

Vol. 9

| Place | Date | Hour | Summary of Events and Information | Remarks and references to Appendices |
|---|---|---|---|---|
| ARMENTIERES | 29/12/16 | | Draft of 6 O.R's departed from base camp. O'Richardson and Caine reported from hospital. During the night our guns continually fired on the enemy's wire. | |
| " | 30/12/16 | | Lieut Ricketts and Pte Ronson proceeded to UK on leave to the 9th Jan/17. M.Gs. were very active throughout the night firing on the Distillery, La Foulloye, and the enemy's communication trenches. | |
| " | 31/12/16 | 11am | Gun teams of 'A' section (1,2,3,4) relieved teams of 'B' section at S.10.19.12 Loisions. 'D' section teams relieved 'C' sec. & whence 'B' in frontline. 'B' whence to C.H.Q. Rue Masle. 4 days rest. | |
| " | " | 10.30am | 'C' section under command of Lieut S.A Crosher attended Divine Service at the Canteen, Rue Masle. | |

J. Morpeth Lieut
O.C. 102. M.G. Coy.

# WAR DIARY

## INTELLIGENCE SUMMARY of No. 102. M.G. Coy.

Vol 10

Army Form C. 2118.

| Place | Date | Hour | Summary of Events and Information | Remarks and references to Appendices |
|---|---|---|---|---|
| ARMENTIERES | 1/1/17 | 9am | Sigs: Hul and Mattock laid a wire from Lilly Post. O.P. to No 7 Gun Position. Our artillery were very active during the day. M/G fire on enemy's wire and communication trenches during the night. | |
| " | 2/1/17 | | During the night our guns were fired on gaps in the enemy's wire and their communication trenches. | |
| " | 3/1/17 | 11am | Lieut. R.H. Thomas reported for duty vice 2 Lt L Bell to 2nd Army School of Instructors. | |
| " | 4/1/17 | 3am | 12913 Pte Baugh died of Pneumonia at No. Casualty Clearing Station. Rebeck took place. "C" Section returned to Coy H.Q for 4 days rest. | |
| " | 5/1/17 | 1pm | Enemy artillery shelled heavily vicinity of Church Chapelle d'armentieres. During the night we carried out usual M.G. fire on enemy's front line also on gaps in the wire. 2000 rounds were fired. | |
| " | 6/1/17 | | Our guns carried out the usual fire, searching the enemy wire and playing on their communication trenches throughout the night. | |
| " | 7/1/17 | | Nothing of note tonight during the day. From 10.15pm to 10.55pm one gun fired indirectly on La Houssoie on | |

Nuthall Lieut
O.C. 102 M.G. Coy.

# WAR DIARY

## INTELLIGENCE SUMMARY

of No: 102nd M.G. Coy.

Army Form C. 2118.

| Place | Date | Hour | Summary of Events and Information | Remarks and references to Appendices |
|---|---|---|---|---|
| ARMENTIERES | 8/-/17 | 11am | Reliefs took place. "D" Section came out for 4 days rest. Q.M. Watson admitted to hospital with bitten ankle. | |
| " | 9th | | The usual firing was carried out by our guns during the night. Sgt Rickit returned from leave. | |
| " | | | During the night M.G. fire was directed on gaps in enemy wire and on enemy communication trenches around Le Touquet. | |
| " | 10th | 11am | Draft of 6 men including Cpl Bentley R. started for duty from Base Depot. The guns fired throughout the night at gaps in the wire etc. | |
| " | 11th | | The day passed very quiet. Guns were firing during the night. | |
| " | 12th | 10am | Reliefs took place. "A" Section returned to H.Q. for 3 days rest. Cpl Jarvis proceeded to U.K. on leave to the 23rd inst. | |
| " | 13th | 10-30am | Cpl Baker L/ transferred to the Base under age. | |
| " | | 11am | Cpl Casey fired by F.G.C.M. In overstaying leave to U.K. 3 days. Between 11am and 12noon enemy dropped 16 shells in trenches E of CHURCH CHAPPE d'ARMENTIERES. During the night we carried out M.G. fire on enemy front line, trench and wire, also gaps cut in the wire. 5000 rounds were fired. | |

U.C. No: 102 M.G. Coy.

Army Form C. 2118.

# WAR DIARY
## INTELLIGENCE SUMMARY
(Erase heading not required.) of No. 102 M.G. Coy.

| Place | Date | Hour | Summary of Events and Information | Remarks and references to Appendices |
|---|---|---|---|---|
| ARMENTIERES | 14/1/17 | | During the day, our artillery were very active. Throughout the night our M.Gs were firing on jobs in the enemy's wire. | |
| " | 15/1/17 | 6am | Cpl Cleven proceeded to ZUYTPEENE. for 6 weeks course of Signalling. | |
| " | " | " | L/C Brown — " — Cameros for Pd 38th M.G. Course till the 2nd Feb: | |
| " | " | 11am | Capt Scott and Lieut Chapple proceeded to the Corps School for 5 days course. | |
| " | " | 2pm | Lieut Anderson, 2nd Roberts reported for duty with the Coy. | |
| " | 16/1/17 | | Owing to the fog we carried out the M.G fire on enemy front line and wire throughout the day. | |
| " | 17/1/17 | | During the night we also fired on enemy line and wire. 5,700 rounds were fired between 12noon and 1am. Enemy dropped about 15 shells in the vicinity of Curb Roads and on ARMENTIERES ROAD, CHAPELLE d'ARMENTIERES. Two damaged guns returned from the line to when No. 3676 damaged was sent back, No. L.2472 broken side plate Blurp; to Armourers shop. We carried out the usual M.G. fire throughout the night. | |
| " | 18/1/17 | 10am | No.60682 O.M. Wright D. proceeded to Bailleu in accordance with A.H. 682 dt 15/1/17. During the night we carried out the usual firing on jobs in the enemy's wire. | |

Whittups Lieut
O.C. 102 M.G. Coy.

T.2134. Wt. W708—776. 500000. 4/15. Sir J. C. & S.

**Army Form C. 2118.**

# WAR DIARY
## or
## INTELLIGENCE SUMMARY.
(Erase heading not required.) **Of No 102 M.G. Coy**

Instructions regarding War Diaries and Intelligence Summaries are contained in F.S. Regs., Part II. and the Staff Manual respectively. Title pages will be prepared in manuscript.

| Place | Date | Hour | Summary of Events and Information | Remarks and references to Appendices |
|---|---|---|---|---|
| ARMENTIERES | 19/2/17 | | No 3678 Gunr returned from Armourers Shop. L/Cpl McKenzie wired on leave to UK vice 2/1/17. Relief took place. C section came out for 3 days rest. To Stiorf Post billets. During the night we carried out M.G. fire on paths, the enemy wire and on communication trenches. | |
| " | 20/2/17 | | Enemy were very active throughout the day. L/Cpl Henley wounded at Lille Post. Pt. Q.S.W. Rifle leg and left fort., died on the way to the A.D.S. Pt. Bentley returned to Coy from No.2 F.A. Our guns fired throughout the whole of the night. L/Cpl Copley wounded in the neck by shrapnel. | |
| " | 21/2/17 | | No other shots received tonight. During the night we carried out M.G. fire on enemy communication around the Distillery La Houssoie, from 10 pm to 9 pm enemy dumps, from 12 M.N. to 6 am 27 d on paths in enemy wire. Also fired on enemy front line. 3450 rounds fired | |
| " | 22/2/17 | | We carried out M.G. fire on enemy front line and fork in the wire also on the DISTILLERY, LA HOUSSOIE, throughout the night. 4250 rounds were fired. | |

J. Whittington
Lieut.
O.C. 102 M.G. Coy

T2134. Wt. W708-776. 500000. 4/15. Sir J.C. & S.

Army Form C. 2118.

# WAR DIARY
## of
## INTELLIGENCE SUMMARY.
(Erase heading not required.) Of the 102 M. G. Coy

Instructions regarding War Diaries and Intelligence Summaries are contained in F. S. Regs., Part II. and the Staff Manual respectively. Title pages will be prepared in manuscript.

| Place | Date | Hour | Summary of Events and Information | Remarks and references to Appendices |
|---|---|---|---|---|
| ARMENTIERES | 23/1/17 | | Our Guns carried out the usual firing throughout the night on paths in the enemy wire and communication trenches | |
| " | 24/1/17 | | Our artillery was very active throughout the day cutting wire. | |
| " | | | Our Guns fired on the paths during the night. | |
| " | 25/1/17 | | Cpls Truesdale and Ormond admitted to 103 F.A. M.B's were firing on enemy communication trenches throughout the night. | |
| " | 26/1/17 | | Pte Williams D admitted to 3rd D.R.S | |
| " | | | During the night M.G's were very active firing on the paths in the wire etc. | |
| " | 27/1/17 | 12 noon | "D" Section went into Subsidiary Line. "A" came out to rest. | |
| " | | 4 pm | The Company were relieved by 10th Australian M.G. Coy. | |
| " | | 11 pm | Left Rue Marle and marched via Erquinghem, Steenwerck, Bailleul, arrived at Meteren about 5.45 am 28th inst | |
| Meteren | 28/1/17 | | Coy left Meteren at 11am and marched to CAESTRE arriving about 3pm. | |
| CAESTRE | | | H.Q. "A" and "B" Section billeted in a farm. "A.C." and "D" in the village | |
| " | | | Pte Enniption returned from the Base. | |
| " | | | Lieut Sawyer joined the Coy. Officers reported multiple tailplanes falling out on the march | |

Whittaker Lt
O.C. 102 M.G. Coy

**WAR DIARY**

**INTELLIGENCE SUMMARY.**
(Erase heading not required.) of No: 102 M.G. Coy.

Army Form C. 2118.

| Place | Date | Hour | Summary of Events and Information | Remarks and references to Appendices |
|---|---|---|---|---|
| CA ESTRE. HEBETEN. | 29/1/17 | 10am | Company paraded at the Farm for inspection of Section Officers, afterwards Lewis limbers and cleaning of guns. | |
| " | | 2pm | Remainder of Coy were paid out | |
| " | 30/1/17 | 9am | Coy paraded for Physical Training | |
| " | | 9.30 | " " " Gun cleaning etc. | |
| " | | 2pm | Rutherick under Lieut Brown till 4pm. | |
| " | 31/1/17 | | Cpl Hilton rejoined from 2nd Army Instructional School Stones. Company paraded during the day for Physical Training etc. | |

Rutherford Lieut
O.C. 102. M.G. Coy

WAR   DIARY

OF

102nd MACHINE GUN COMPANY.


MONTH - FEBRUARY, 1917.

# WAR DIARY
## or
## INTELLIGENCE SUMMARY

Army Form C. 2118.

| Place | Date | Hour | Summary of Events and Information | Remarks and references to Appendices |
|---|---|---|---|---|
| CAESAR | 1/12/17 | pm | Co. commanders on leave on ... | |
| | | 10.30 | Army Commander inspected billets at 11 & afternoon interview | |
| | | 6.30 | ... | |
| | | | "D" Squadron on route march ret ... | |
| | 2/12/17 | | 2 guns sent to gun range. | |
| | | | Men at court martial trial for money. | |
| | | 12.30 | Ordered to leave billets, leaving shot horses. | |
| | 3/12/17 | am | The usual brigade parade was cancelled. | |
| | | 2.30 | Fervent two teams of "B" delivered "C" Lee. and two teams of ? | |
| | | | on anti aircraft duties. | |
| | 4/12/17 | | Brigade paraded dismount the march to open civil etc. | |
| | | 2.30 pm | Paraded for route march returned about 4.30 p.m. | |
| | 5/12/17 | 9-12 | Coy carried out usual parades including instruction on German M.G. | |
| | | 1 to 4 | ditto ditto. Anti Balloon gun anti aircraft duties by 15th M.G. Coy ... | |

J. Fitzgerald
Lt. R.C.D. Fitzgerald pro

Army Form C. 2118.

# WAR DIARY
## or
## INTELLIGENCE SUMMARY.

(Erase heading not required.) Of No. 102. M. G. Coy.

Instructions regarding War Diaries and Intelligence Summaries are contained in F. S. Regs., Part II. and the Staff Manual respectively. Title pages will be prepared in manuscript.

| Place | Date | Hour | Summary of Events and Information | Remarks and references to Appendices |
|---|---|---|---|---|
| CAESTRE | 6/1/17 | 9 am | Company Commanders Conference Attending. Brig. Cocker spoke. | |
| | | 11-130 | Snowing when out. Shall have artillery as to be hostile. | |
| | | | "B" Sec baled. | |
| | | 2.30 | Coy. Lunches for Brigade route march returned at 4.15 pm | |
| | 7/1/17 | | Usual programme of work was carried out during the morning | |
| | | 2.30 | Coy Team played a friendly football match with 102 F.A. Coy R.A.M.C. Lost 6-0. | |
| | 8/1/17 | 9 am | Coy took part in a Brigade route march to THIEUSOUX, FLETRE returning to billets about 11 am | |
| | | 12.30 | Remainder of the Company bathed. | |
| | | | St Richell O/C Coy. and Donaldson admitted to hospital. | |
| | 9/1/17 | 4 pm | Usual Company Parades. | |
| | | 8 pm | Company Smoking concert baked. | |
| | 10/1/17 | 9-12 | "A" and "B" Sections fired on the Range. Lectures of S.A.A. to section before fired | |
| | | 2-4 | "C" and "D" Sections fired on the Range. | |

Hazebrouck Bys
O.C. No. 102 M.G. Coy.

# WAR DIARY

## INTELLIGENCE SUMMARY.

(Erase heading not required.) of 740:102. M.G. Col.

Army Form C. 2118.

| Place | Date | Hour | Summary of Events and Information | Remarks and references to Appendices |
|---|---|---|---|---|
| CAESTRE | 11/8/17 | 9am 1pm | Route march - Croix Rouge St Pequelen and on to Caestre Lecture | |
| " | 12/8/17 | | During the morning the company had a run on the range. In the afternoon a demonstration was given by the Anti-Gas officer. O'Brien and Vickery passed | |
| " | 13/8/17 | | In the morning the Coy passed out but not the numbers at a limber drill | |
| " | 14/8/17 | 2-4pm 6-8 2-4 | Company drill on big football field. C.Q.M.S Dean to R.F.C H.Q. "A" and "B" Section on the range. Y l rounds fired. " " " " " " " " " " "C" and "D" " " " " " " Pl twenty returned from leave. | |
| " | 15/8/17 | am | Sergt Smith transferred to R.F.C. H.Q. on probation. Usual Company parades during the day | |
| " | 16/8/17 | 10-12 9.1. | Company fired on the range. Lut Ludwin returned from leave Limbers were also licked | |
| " | 17/8/17 | 9-10 2-4 | Company turn out with clothing afterwards carried out Gun Drill Company Drill | Rutherfer Lieut O.C. 102. M.G.C. |

# WAR DIARY or INTELLIGENCE SUMMARY

Army Form C. 2118.

| Place | Date | Hour | Summary of Events and Information | Remarks and references to Appendices |
|---|---|---|---|---|
| CAESTRE | 18/6/17 | 11am | Company left CAESTRE and marched via HAZEBROUCK to (Estree) MORBECQUE and detrained for the night. | |
| MORBECQUE | 19th | 8.30 | Left for MAZINGHAM arriving at 2.30pm. Billeted in one M.P.T. | |
| MAZINGHAM | 20th | " | Left for THIEULOYE arriving in M.P.T. and bivouac. Platoons | |
| | | | arriving at COESREVILLE. | |
| COESREVILLE | 21st | 9am | Arrived and to ECOIVRES. arrived about 11am and billeted in M.P.T. | |
| ECOIVRES | 22nd | | Coy remained in Mt. St Eloi & Gr Ridge and has worked from Jonstay. | |
| " " | 23rd | | Left for ARRAS at 2.30pm arriving at 5.30pm. SS Hud to Hospital. | |
| ARRAS | " | | "A", "B" and "C" Sections relieved Sections of 24 N.E. Coy in the line. | |
| " | 24th | | HQ and "D" Section (in reserve) billeted in the RUE-DE-FOUR. | |
| " | 25th 6am | | D. Section under Sg. Callaghan carried Pim teams returns to the dumps. | |
| " | 25th 6pm | | 500 rounds fired at H 7 & 40. and at H 13 & 45. | |
| " | | 12md | 300 " " H 7 & 40 " H 13 & 45. | |
| " | 26th 5.30am | | Division on left raided enemy trenches. No G gun close by to | |
| | | | fire on suitable targets, were presented. Enemy retaliated vigorously with artillery | |

Army Form C. 2118.

102 M.G. Coy.

# WAR DIARY
or
# INTELLIGENCE SUMMARY.
(Erase heading not required.)

| Place | Date | Hour | Summary of Events and Information | Remarks and references to Appendices |
|---|---|---|---|---|
| ARRAS | 24/2/17 | 5.10 p.m. | 2/Lieut. L. Newsome and L/Cpl. Hogue returned from G.H.Q. Ebert, Cameron. Went to Brigade (25th) on our right handed enemy trenches. Our No. 2 gun (at H.Q. M.E.P.) was firing in support of a Battalion M.G. in LAURENT BLANGY G.R.6.g.S.25. Gun at No. 10 M.G.P. fired 500 rounds during the night at H.16.q.g.5. a point where relief into trenches. Similar had fired from R.13.c.10 to B.13.c.69 was freely shelled also – 730 rounds expended. Gun at No. 9 M.G. position is in a disused trench off October Avenue. The trench was deepened where it leads into October Avenue. During raid mentioned above enemy sent up Red lights along the whole line, but several green rockets were fired from the central sector roads. After every burst fired during the raid from No. 9 position a stream of bullets from enemy M.G. faced over the gun. Evidently the position has been spotted before its Coy. took over from the 24th M.G.Coy. Enemy retaliation to raid lasted one hour – mostly stuff long-wood. | |
| | 26.2.17 | Noon. | Sgt Callaghan, Pt Wright, Lt Palmer proceeded to course on Identification of Aeroplanes at Anti-Aircraft Battery that WARLUS. | |

Nutching Lt
O.C. 102 M.G. Coy.

Army Form C. 2118.

# WAR DIARY
## INTELLIGENCE SUMMARY.
*(Erase heading not required.)*

102. M.G. Coy.

Vol XI

| Place | Date | Hour | Summary of Events and Information | Remarks and references to Appendices |
|---|---|---|---|---|
| ARRAS | 1/3/17 | 4 pm | O/C 2nd Lieut Winnie from 104 S.A. C/o Briggs and Allison wounded (C.S. Wood later died of wounds). Enemy shoot fort the night as on previous night. No casualties. 2/Lt Henson joined his section with Brens. | |
| | 2/3/17 | | Machine gun fire was directed on the Railway B 26 C and on ROAD H 1 a 9 3, BOIS de la MAISON BLANCHE. | |
| | 3/3/17 | 1 am | 1000 rounds fired on A 30 d 9.4. | |
| | | 5:30 am | | |
| | | 6-9 | Vertical searching on ROAD from A 24 b 40 00 to B 13 b 10 50. | |
| | | 10 am | "D" section relieved "A" section at positions 9, 10, 11, 12, on nights of sector. 2/Lt Owen relieved Lt Anderson. | |
| | | 6 pm | L/Cpl Hayton and Ptes Wilde, Worth and Wilkinson reported today from Base Depot. | |
| | | 3 am | During hostile shelling a 4.2 how smashed up emplacement at no. 9 position. Infact was uninjured. | |

[signature] 6 Aug

# WAR DIARY
## or
## INTELLIGENCE SUMMARY of No 102 M.G. Coy.

Army Form C. 2118.

| Place | Date | Hour | Summary of Events and Information | Remarks and references to Appendices |
|---|---|---|---|---|
| ARRAS. | 3 3.17 | 6a 10.30p.m | No.10 Gun fired on H.1.b.65 where track leaves railway between 6 and 10.30 p.m. Retaliation with left shrapnel about twenty yds to left of gun. Other targets were BAHNEIN SCHITT (B26c); railway from H.1.b POPO to forked road H.1.a.9.3. G.26.c.50.30. | Map Ref. 51/a NW 1 ROCKLINCOURT. 1/10,000. 51/a NW 3 ARRAS 1:10,000 |
| | 4.3.17 | 5 p.m | 2/Lt B.B. CRAPPLE returned from trenches to Coy H.Q. sick. 47st BAHNEIN SCHITT and forked road H.1.a.9.3 freely sprinkled with fire. No indirect fire carried out by "B" section owing to lays working parties near Gun Positions. | |
| | | 7.10 | Our a/Aa 9 position fired on H.1.d 35.50 and No 11 Gun at H.1.b.77. - 2000 rounds expended. | |
| | 5.3.17 | 6 a.m | A few 15 cm shells fell behind No 9 position; a few shells & various sizes near Guns of "B" section. Major Mellaby of 103 M.G. Coy visited Coy.H.Q. to arrange details of relief. | |

Matthews P/ps
O.C. 102 M.G. Coy

Army Form C. 2118.

# WAR DIARY
## INTELLIGENCE SUMMARY of 162 M.G. Coy
*(Erase heading not required.)*

Instructions regarding War Diaries and Intelligence Summaries are contained in F.S. Regs., Part II. and the Staff Manual respectively. Title pages will be prepared in manuscript.

| Place | Date | Hour | Summary of Events and Information | Remarks and references to Appendices |
|---|---|---|---|---|
| ARRAS | 5-3-17 | 6-8 am | Proceeded on B.25 c B.20.30 and B.19.d.20.70. | Ref Sheet 51B NW1 ROCLINCOURT 1:10000 51B NW 3 ARRAS 1:10,000 |
| | | 7-7.30 | Railway on B.26.c searched. | |
| | | 9.15-10.45 | Enemy shelled C.T.; no enemy in sun positions. his harassing fire positions completed at No 2 position; crew one stated at No 10. Chalk from shells at 10 km. | |
| | | 7.30-8 pm | H.1.a.29 freely sprinkled. | |
| | 6-3-17 | 5-4.30 am | Railway in B.26.c searched, and Iron Road H.1.a.9.3 also. | |
| | | 9 pm | Corpl. (a duty) OAKLEY and Yeoman 1kg.1y proceeded to transport lines en route for AUBIGNY. | |
| | | | A working party of 50 men proceeded to trenches at 9 am to hold cold to be obtained as party returned the same party proceeded to work at 3 pm. | |
| | 7/3/17 | 9 am | A working party of 20 men under Corpl Hutchins proceeded to the trenches returned about 11 pm. | |
| | | 4h-8h - 1.30 am | Pvt Lahm firstly trained again at the OCTROI as guide and carried party to 163 M.G. Coy | J. Rutherford Lieutenant O.C. 162 M.G. Coy |

Army Form C. 2118.

Army Form C. 2118.

# WAR DIARY
## or
## INTELLIGENCE SUMMARY of 162. M.G. Coy

(Erase heading not required.)

| Place | Date | Hour | Summary of Events and Information | Remarks and references to Appendices |
|---|---|---|---|---|
| ARRAS. | 8/3/17 | 6.30 am | Company marched to ECOIVRES arriving about 9.30 am. Transfer guns remain in the line under Mr Teostone against beyond of 8th Division under Mr Anderson left by bus for DIEVAL | |
| ECOIVRES | " | 6am | | |
| " | 9/3/17 | " | Remainder of the Coy proceeded to DIEVAL by buses. | |
| DIEVAL | 10/3/17 | | The day was spent in general cleaning of guns etc, checking of equipts. | |
| " | 11/3/17 | 9.30 | Non Conformists attended Divine Service at YMCA hut. | |
| " | " | 9.30 | RC's attended Church, YMCA hut. | |
| " | 12/3/17 | 11am | Inspection of the Brigade by Sir Chas. Ferguson Comdg 17th A.C. | |
| " | " | | Lieut Col Hutchins promoted Sergt-ree Mulder with 4/6/16. Presentation of medal ribbons in course of Identification of awards. Lieut Col Taylor proceeded to MARLES about 3pm. | |
| " | 2/3/17 | 9am | Brigade field day boy returned to billets about 3pm. | |
| " | 13/3/17 | 9am | Somers billeted at ROLLECORT. 6 Section attended Brigade field day. 4 Guns were taken. The Section returned at 2.15pm. | |

JHutchinson Lieut
O.C. 162 M.G. Coy

# WAR DIARY
## or
## INTELLIGENCE SUMMARY.

Army Form C. 2118.

*(Erase heading not required.)* No. 102. M. G. Coy.

| Place | Date | Hour | Summary of Events and Information | Remarks and references to Appendices |
|---|---|---|---|---|
| DIEVAL | 14/3/17 | 9 am | Whole Company turned to Brigade field day. Returning about 2-30 pm. | |
| " | 15/3/17 | " | 'D' Section attended field day. | |
| " | " | 8.15 | 'A' Section on the range. | |
| " | " | 9 pm | 'B' Section turned for care and cleaning. "B" Section bathed at 10 am. | |
| " | 16/3/17 | 9 am | Coy attended field day. 2Lt Mitchell joined Coy. Cpl. O'R Maddock off. It had cancelled. | |
| " | 17-3-17 | 9 am | 'B' Section turned for Brigade field day. | |
| " | " | 9 am | 100 pm teams with Luis Andrson proceed to SAVY BERLETTE STATION for Anti aircraft duties. Transport and remainder of the Coy to find "C" and "D" Sections instruction on the German gun. | |
| " | 18/3/17 | 10 am | 2Lieut Roberts left to join 153 M.G. Coy. 2Lt Thomas to course of Identification of Aeroplanes. 'B' Section on field day. Returned at 4 pm. | |
| " | 19/3/17 | 9 am | 'B' Section attended field day. 'B' Section cleaning guns etc 10 men bathed. | |
| " | 20/3/17 | 6 pm | Company left DIEVAL for BETHONSART. Arriving about 8 pm. | |
| Bethonsart | 21/2/17 | 9 am | Left to LOUEZ, arrival at 2 pm. | |
| LOUEZ | 22/3/17 | 9 pm | A body party of 50 men proceed to the trenches to relieve gun emplacements. Returned at 6 am. 23rd. | |

J. Rutledge
O.C. 102 M.G. Coy

Army Form C. 2118.

# WAR DIARY
## or
## INTELLIGENCE SUMMARY.
(Erase heading not required.)

of No 162 M.C. Coy

| Place | Date | Hour | Summary of Events and Information | Remarks and references to Appendices |
|---|---|---|---|---|
| LOUEZ | 23/3/17 | 9 pm | Working party of 56 went to the line to continue the work with the emplacements etc. Returned about 5 a.m. 24th. Pte Trelethan and Llewellin rejoined the Company. | |
| " | 24/3/17 | 8.45 | Another working party proceeded to the line, returning at 6 am 25th. Cpl Southgate wounded from hospital. Pte Rider returned from hospital U.K. | |
| " | 25/3/17 | 8/9 pm | A working party of 50 men again went to work on emplacements | |
| " | 26/3/17 | 5.30 pm | A working party of 50 men continued to work on emplacements returning at 2 am. | |
| | | 9 pm | A party of 16 went as carrying party to the line | |
| " | 27/3/17 | 5.30 | Working parties continued as on the 26th inst. | |
| | | 9 pm | | |
| " | 28/3/17 | 5 pm | The actual working and carrying parties proceeded to the line | |
| | | 9 pm | Returning about 2 am. Sergts Ellis, Pyke, Trebell, Johnson posted from the Base. | |
| " | 29/3/17 | | 60 men from Battalion from 20th, 21st, 22nd, 23rd N.F.'s alloted for duty at carrying party | |
| " | 30/3/17 | 9 pm | A carrying party of 95 men proceeded to the line under Lieut Dixon | |

# WAR DIARY
## or
## INTELLIGENCE SUMMARY.
(Erase heading not required.) of No: 102: M.G. Coy.

Army Form C. 2118.

| Place | Date | Hour | Summary of Events and Information | Remarks and references to Appendices |
|---|---|---|---|---|
| LOUEZ | 31/3/17 | 9/pm | A working party of 56 men proceeded to the trenches to continued with the work on the emplacements etc. | |

Hutchinson Lieut.
O.C. 102. M.G. Coy

(6202) W 11186/M1151 350,000 12/16 McA. & W., Ltd. (Est. 781) Forms/W 3091/3. Army Form W. 3091.

## Cover for Documents.

Nature of Enclosures.

# WAR DIARY.

## APRIL. 1917.

### 102ND MACHINE GUN COMPANY.

Notes, or Letters written.

# WAR DIARY
## INTELLIGENCE SUMMARY of 102 Machine Gun Coy.

Army Form C. 2118.

| Place | Date | Hour | Summary of Events and Information | Remarks and references to Appendices |
|---|---|---|---|---|
| Louez | 1/4/17 | | 2nd Lieut. Offery and 2 O.R's returned for duty from Base Depot. Working party went up into trenches at night, returning in morning, completing the work on special saps and emplacements at G.5.b. * Diagram of saps attached marked Appendix I. Party of 14 minors moved into trenches to complete dugouts for the company. | Diagram of saps attached + marked Appendix I. * Sheet 51B. |
| " | 2/4/17 | | C Section under Lieut Stevenson moved from Athies, Ecoivres to Louez. Working party carried S.A.A. into the trenches. | |
| " | 3/4/17 | | B, C Sections and 2 Gun teams of D Section with attached N.F. men moved into trenches as part of Trench Garrison, relieving teams of no __ Machine Gun Company. Working party carried S.A.A. into trenches. | |
| Ecoivres | 5/4/17 | | Remainder of Company moved to Mulvents, Ecoivres. Programme of Harvest fire (in accordance with Divisional orders) commenced, on selected Targets, by French Garrison. | |
| | 6/4/17 | | Miners and 2 teams of D Section returned to Company H.Q. under 2nd Lieut R Tansen. Harvest fire continued by A + B sections throughout day and night. Trench garrison positions heavily shelled. Lt Weitz A. wounded. Indirect fire emplacement at G.5.b. 56.70 destroyed by shell. Gun withdrawn, otherwise __ great __ | |

H. Walkington
O.C. 102 Machine Gun Coy.

# WAR DIARY
# INTELLIGENCE SUMMARY

Army Form C. 2118.

of 102 M.G. Coy.

(Erase heading not required.)

Instructions regarding War Diaries and Intelligence Summaries are contained in F.S. Regs., Part II. and the Staff Manual respectively. Title pages will be prepared in manuscript.

| Place | Date | Hour | Summary of Events and Information | Remarks and references to Appendices |
|---|---|---|---|---|
| 6/4/17 Ecoivres | 6/4/17 | | No damage or casualties. D Section had baths. | |
| | 7/4/17 | | 8 O.R.'s reported from Base de pot. Section bathed. A & D Sections are attached N.F. new and headquarters moved into trenches. Headquarters in dugout at Aureux Avenue; C section under 102 Brigade; remainder of Coy under D.M.G.O. Lieut Rutherford to Transport, stores etc. and Sergt. Coustru & 36 O.R. left behind remained at Ecoivres for the night. | |
| | 8/4/19 | | Transport & details left behind moved to Y Huttments on Arras. St Pol Road at L.8.c.60.90. Sheet 51C. No accommodation found for men, so makeshift shelters made for the night. Transport lines at ETRUN. | M.G.4. 51.C. |
| | | 7.p.m. | 16 Pack Mules sent to Rocluncourt and attached to D.A.C. All Gun teams of A, B, & D Sections took up their positions in the special laps at G.S.B central, and "South." | |
| | 9/4/17 | 4.30 a.m. | Guns laid on their Barrage Targets.* | |
| | | 5.30 a.m. | Infantry assault on enemy positions commences. | |
| | | 5.15 a.m. | Machine Gun barrage opened by A, B, D Sections in accordance with Divisional Scheme.* | * Barrage targets + time table shewn on attached Map respectively, + Appendix I + II respectively. |

[signature]
O.C. 102 M.G. Coy.

# WAR DIARY
## of 102 M.G. Coy.
## INTELLIGENCE SUMMARY

Army Form C. 2118.

| Place | Date | Hour | Summary of Events and Information | Remarks and references to Appendices |
|---|---|---|---|---|
| | 9/4/17 | 5.25 a.m. | C Section "stood to" in dugouts ready to move forward to hold captured positions on receiving orders from Brigade headquarters. | |
| | | 8 a.m. | C Section (4 guns) under Lieut J. Newsome moved forward and took up defensive positions in Blue Line. Barrage by A.B. & D Sections left at 1011 been when guns ceased fire. Infantry assault highly successful, and all objectives taken according to time table, with less casualties. Many known machine guns and field guns taken. All ranks of this unit carried out their duties in a highly creditable manner and the guns worked excellently; all prisoners spoke as to the effectiveness of M/c machine Gun Barrages. Little artillery barrage reply. Casualties as follows. Killed – 108 – 12897 Pte Hopkin W. Wounded 4 O.R's ing – 53037 Sergt Pryke A.F.L. 5236 A/Cpl Redpath R, 15299 Pte Luck J. 12897 McLoughlin J. gassed by carbon monoxide fumes from gun blowing back. | |
| | | 1 p.m. | A Section (Lt Ltd Anderson + 2nd Lt R.H. Thomas) and D Section (2nd Lieut R.O. Tower) moves forward to defensive positions in Blue Line: B Section (2nd Lt Dixon + B.St.Leary) remained in dugouts near Ecops on Divisional Reserve. Forward Coy. Headquarters in Blue Line, Coy. Sgt. Major, 2 Signallers + Artificer remained at Bn Headquarters in Lawrence Avenue. | |

Nutt Lt
O.C. 102 M.G. Coy.

**Army Form C. 2118.**

# WAR DIARY
# or
# INTELLIGENCE SUMMARY

of 102 M.G. Coy.

*(Erase heading not required.)*

Instructions regarding War Diaries and Intelligence Summaries are contained in F. S. Regs., Part II. and the Staff Manual respectively. Title pages will be prepared in manuscript.

| Place | Date | Hour | Summary of Events and Information | Remarks and references to Appendices |
|---|---|---|---|---|
| Y Hill | 10/4/17 | | Accommodation found for lorries + details in Y Hill L.S.E. to 9.0. Drafts of B.O.R's sent up line to replace Casualties. Two Gun Teams of C Section under Lieut J.C. Heart were moved forward from Blue to Brown line. Remaining two teams of C Section remained in Blue line. | |
| | 11/4/17 | | D Section (4 guns) under 2nd Lieut R.T. Owen moved forward from Blue to Brown line. Two teams of "B" Section under Lieut H.G. Anderson moved forward from Blue to Brown line. Remaining two teams of "B" Section remained in Blue line. Disposition of Guns therefore as follows:- In Brown line – 8 guns; In Blue line – 4 guns; In Divisional Reserve – 4 guns. Casualty – Wounded 1.O.R. No 8/2415 Pte Watt A.A. A & C Sections Gun teams in Brown line were relieved and moved by the remaining teams of their Respective Sections. The teams relieved moved back to the positions in Blue line vacated by the teams who relieved them. Disposition Vacifies as for 10th. Casualty ; Wounded 1.O.R. 12836 Pte Render J. | |
| | 12/4/17 | | B Section (2nd (Gun Swarn T B.A.(erry)) moved forward to Brown line. Two teams of "A" Section + Hm Blue line, Two teams of "A" Section relieved two teams of "A" in Brown line, the latter returning to Divisional Reserve. | |

J. Stewart Lieut. for
O.C. 102 M.G. Coy.

T./134. Wt. W708-776. 500 000. 4/15. Sir J. C. & S.

# WAR DIARY or INTELLIGENCE SUMMARY

Army Form C. 2118.

| Place | Date | Hour | Summary of Events and Information | Remarks and references to Appendices |
|---|---|---|---|---|
| | 12/4/17 | | Two teams of C Section moved forward from Blue line relieving two teams of C Section. The latter moving forward to position in Green line. Disposition as follows:- In Green line - 2 guns: In Brown line 10 guns: In Divisional Reserve 4 guns. Casualties: Wounded 1 off. Sergt J. Newsome (Shock) O.R.; 2: 85266 Cpl McCall P. 85319 Pte Haines R.J. | |
| | 13/3/17 | | Transport details moved up to LES QUATRE VENTS, ST NICHOLAS: The two teams of C Section in Green line took up position in Brown line, otherwise disposition as for 12th. | |
| | 14/4/17 | | Coy relieved by no 190 Machine Gun Coy, and returned to Transport lines for the night. 16 Pack Mules returned to Coy from O.R.C. | |
| | 15/4/17 | | Company marched to the OCTROI, ARRAS and embussed for LA THIEULOYE: Billeted in Barns. | |
| LA THIEULOYE | 16/4/17 | | Cleaning of Clothing &c: Inspection of Clothing & equipment. | |
| -"- | 17/4/17 | | Box Respirator & gas helmet inspection: Cleaning of guns & gun equipment. | |
| -"- | 18/4/17 | | Squad drill, cleaning of kits &c. | |
| -"- | 19/4/17 | | Company inspected by XVII Corps Commander, and speeches commenced for the fine work done by the company in the attack on 9/4/17 | |

K Rutherford Lieut for
O.C. 102 M.G. Coy.

Army Form C. 2118.

# WAR DIARY
## or
## INTELLIGENCE SUMMARY.
*(Erase heading not required.)*

No. 102 M.G.Coy.

| Place | Date | Hour | Summary of Events and Information | Remarks and references to Appendices |
|---|---|---|---|---|
| LA THIEULOYE | 30/3/17 | | Lieut G.S. Blenberg returned for duty from Base Depôt. | |
| " | 21/4/17 | | Gun drill, gun cleaning, etc. | |
| ACQ | 21/4/17 | 9.a.m. | Marched off to take up at ACQ. | |
| LA RESSETT. | 22/4/17 | 6 p.m. | Marched to LA RESSETT. Coy billeted in mill. | |
| | 23/4/17 | | 19 O.R. to be left behind when front A. Coy moved to FREVENT CAPELLE Remainder of Coy stays by awaiting orders. | |
| | 24/4/17 | 4.30 a.m. | Marched off to ARRAS. Coy billeted in RUE DES CHARIOTTES. Transport and | |
| ARRAS. | | | water in Museum Ground | |
| | | 10.30 p.m. | Company and fighting limbers moved up into reserve in old BLACK LINE at about: C.18a. 90.30. to C.12.d. 90.70.: fighting limbers unable to come at C.18.a. 90.20 unless front of battalion. | ~ Map Sheet 51.B |
| | 25/4/17 | | Sited and remainder of Transport moved up to ST NICHOLAS, at C.12.C. 60.50.* | |
| | 26/4/17 | | Details left behind at FREVENT CAPELLE moved up to transport lines. | |

MAY.

**WAR DIARY of N° 102 M.G. Coy.**

Army Form C. 2118.

INTELLIGENCE SUMMARY

(Erase heading not required.)

Instructions regarding War Diaries and Intelligence Summaries are contained in F. S. Regs., Part II. and the Staff Manual respectively. Title pages will be prepared in manuscript.

VOL XIV

Vol 13

| Place | Date | Hour | Summary of Events and Information | Remarks and references to Appendices |
|---|---|---|---|---|
| | 26/4/17 | | Orders were received for guns to move up on the evening of the 27th in readiness for attack on the morning of the 28th | Map reference Sheet 51st NW |
| | 27/4/17 | | In accordance with orders received Capts W.L. Scott & all Section Commanders (Lieut. J. Anderson, 2nd Lt. Mr. Dixon, 2nd Lt. R.A. Thomas, a 2nd Lt. R. Bowen) went forward in the morning and reconnoitred with the Divisional M.G. Officer | |
| | | 6 pm | "A" "B" + "C" Sections moved forward to positions selected under Divisional Barrage Scheme in which two Sections from 101 M.G. Coy. & two Sections from 103 M.G. Coy. were Co-operating. | |
| | | 11.30 pm | D Section moved with 102nd Brigade Infantry to position of readiness in PIKE TRENCH H 16 d. 3. 1. | |
| | | | The Gun positions of A. B + C Sections stretched along a rough line from H.23.B.36.12. to H.23.d.55.80 at irregular intervals. B+C Sections fired from emplacements cut in eastern bank of cutting and 30 yards to right. A Section from shell holes in front of cutting and 30 yards to right of positions in cutting. The Guns were all laid on their Barrage lines by 9 p.m. the remainder of the night being | |

J. Rutherford Lieut.
for O.C. 102 M.G. Coy.

# WAR DIARY of No. 102 M.G. Coy.

## INTELLIGENCE SUMMARY

Vol IV

Army Form C. 2118.

| Place | Date | Hour | Summary of Events and Information | Remarks and references to Appendices |
|---|---|---|---|---|
| | 27/4/17 | | Spent in improving existing cover and getting up S.A.A. from Divisional M.G. S.A.A. Dump. Battle limbers returned to Transport of Details Camp at G.16.b.6.5. | See reference sheet 51 S.N.W. |
| | 28/4/17 | 4 am | XVIII Corps attack on German front System commenced. According to programme guns of A, B, & C Sections placed a fixed barrage on ROEUX from 4 am to 4.25 a.m. On ceasing fire A Section entered cutting and made all preparations to move forward and give supporting fire in case of a successful advance was not achieved. The attack on the 34th Division front failed: B & C Sections therefore stood by ready to fire from their emplacements. Information was received that the enemy was reinforcing across the open country west of the road running north from ROEUX to ARRAS-DOUAI RAILWAY, fire was brought to bear on this during the night. 40,000 Rounds were fired by the 12 guns during the operations and the improvement due to the new MkI Barrels and a muzzle cup was most marked. Practically all stoppages which occurred were due to defective S.A.A. | |

J. Nutbush
O.C. 102 M.G. Coy.
Lieut.

# WAR DIARY

## INTELLIGENCE SUMMARY of No. 102 M.G. Coy

Army Form C. 2118.

| Place | Date | Hour | Summary of Events and Information | Remarks and references to Appendices |
|---|---|---|---|---|
| | 28/4/17 | | Retaliation was slight and in the form of Artillery searching fire. Covering fire was also given to an attack on CHEMICAL WORKS by 102 Brigade, - attack unsuccessful. | Map reference Sheet 51B NW |
| | 29/4/17 | | There was a marked decrease in artillery activity throughout today. At 4pm orders were received that A Section (Lt Anderson) and D Section (2nd Lieut R.P.Owen) to relieve 8 guns of 103rd M.G. Coy in front again in 11.30 pm but 102nd Brigade issued orders that A Section would remain in reserve at Brigade Sqrs H.16.R.7.8. The remaining 4 guns of 103 M.G. Coy being relieved by 4 guns under Battalion arrangements. All guns of B + C Sections carried out intense indirect fire on the same targets as on the night of 28/4/17 each gun firing over 3000 rounds. Retaliation was heavy but there were no casualties. | |
| | 30/4/17 | | Guns in CADIS TRENCH (D Section) had been much troubled by snipers throughout the night and at 1:30 am 2nd Lieut R.P.Owen was shot through the forehead and died at about 3 o'clock without recovering consciousness. 2nd Lieut R.P.Owen lost. Command of D Section vice 2ndLt R.P.Owen killed. | |
| | | 11 am | A + D Sections were relieved by part of no 11 M.G. Coy 4th Div." | |

J. Rothery Lieut
for O.C. 102 M.G. Coy

Appendix I to War Diary
of 102 M G Coy 1st April 1917

Diagram of Saps. used for special barrage 9/4/17.
102 M. G. Coy.

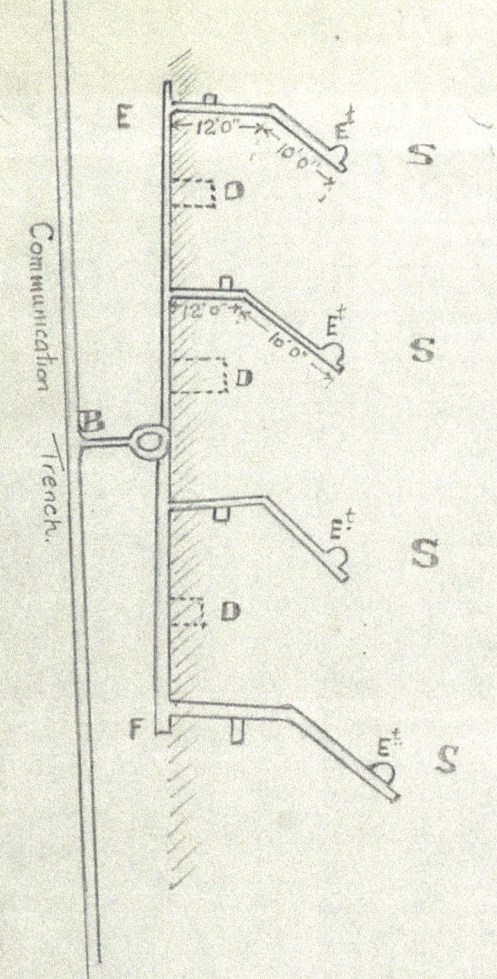

B = Entrance to Sap System from Communication Trench.
EF = Communication Trench in rear of Saps. 4' deep.
D = Small Dugouts for Belt filling
S = Saps. with M.G. emplacements.
E⁺ = Machine Gun Emplacements.

W 5696—2199  50,000  7/15  H W V (M127)

## Certificate to be Signed before Fire is Opened.

1. I have checked all calculations and line of fire of gun.

2. The Brigadier-General commanding the line of trenches, *i.e.*, Nos. _____, has sanctioned fire from _____ to _____ date.

3. The troops occupying trenches No. _____ have been notified.

                        (Signed) _____ B. M. G. O.

Officer in charge of Gun _____  Sheet _____  Square _____

Appendix III
Re Turning.

| PHASE | Nº 1 Gun | Nº 2 Gun | Nº 3 Gun | Nº 4 Gun | Nº 5 Gun | Nº 6 Gun | Nº 7 Gun | Nº 8 Gun | Nº 9 Gun | Nº 10 Gun | Nº 11 Gun | Nº 12 Gun |
|---|---|---|---|---|---|---|---|---|---|---|---|---|
| A. | 63°<br>1900'×<br>3°53'<br>Traverse to<br>Right 1° | 112°×<br>1925'<br>3°33'<br>Traverse to<br>Right 1° | 90°<br>1875'×<br>3°30'<br>Concentrated | 75°<br>2325'×<br>6°8'<br>Concentrated | 53°<br>2375'×<br>6°49'<br>Concentrated | 80°<br>1925'<br>3°45'<br>Concentrated | 84°<br>1875'×<br>3°32'<br>Traverse to<br>Right 1° | 109°<br>1875'×<br>3°20'<br>Concentrated 120°(100×) Right 1° | 64°<br>2025'×<br>4°29'<br>Traverse to Right 1° | 77°<br>2025'×<br>4°17'<br>Concentrated | 47°<br>1875'×<br>3°52'<br>Concentrated | 46°<br>1650'×<br>2°59'<br>Traverse to Right 1° |
| B. | 60°<br>1750'×<br>3°15'<br>3°41'<br>Traverse to Right 1° | 50°×<br>1800'<br>3°41'<br>Traverse to Right 1° | 48°×<br>1800'<br>3°41'<br>Traverse to Right 1° | 39°<br>2100'×<br>5°01'<br>Traverse to Right 1° | | 65°<br>2125'×<br>5°6'<br>Concentrated | 56°<br>1700'×<br>3°5'<br>Traverse to Right 1° | 53°×<br>1700'<br>3°5'<br>Traverse to Right 1° | 60°<br>1600'×<br>2°41'<br>Traverse to Right 1° | 58°<br>1600'×<br>2°43'<br>Traverse to Right 1° | 48°<br>1875'×<br>3°53'<br>Traverse to Right 1° | -ditto- |
| C. | 74°<br>2050'×<br>4°29'<br>Vertical lands<br>+50'/+150' | | | | 73°×<br>2125'<br>4°55'<br>Concentrated | | | 71°<br>1675'×<br>3°45'<br>Vertical lands 125'(100×) | | | | 83°<br>1775'×<br>4°45'<br>Vertical Barrage 125'(100×) |
| D. | 70°<br>2350'×<br>6°27'<br>Traverse to Right 1° | 71°×<br>2350'<br>6°25'<br>Traverse to Right 1° | 73°<br>2350'×<br>6°25'<br>Traverse to Right 1° | 83°<br>2250'×<br>5°33'<br>Traverse to Right 1° | 81°<br>2250'×<br>5°36'<br>Traverse to Right 1° | 80°<br>2750'×<br>5°38'<br>Traverse to Right 1° | 77°<br>2250'×<br>5°41'<br>Traverse to Right 1° | 78°<br>2325'×<br>5°28'<br>Traverse to Right 1° | 76°<br>2325'×<br>5°31'<br>Traverse to Right 1° | 73°<br>2325'×<br>5°31'<br>Traverse to Right 1° | 80°<br>2350'×<br>5°22'<br>Traverse to Right 1° | 77°<br>2175'×<br>5°15'<br>Traverse to Right 1° |
| E. | 77°<br>2825'×<br>10°31'<br>Traverse to Right 1° | 76°×<br>2825'<br>10°31'<br>Traverse to Right 1° | 82°<br>2750'×<br>9°41'<br>Traverse to Right 1° | 83°×<br>2750'<br>9°41'<br>Traverse to Right 1° | 79°<br>2800'×<br>10°10'<br>Traverse to Right 2° | 79°<br>2800'×<br>10°10'<br>Traverse to Right 2° | 81°<br>2825'×<br>10°27'<br>Traverse to Right 2° | 75°<br>2800'×<br>10°14'<br>Traverse to R. 4° | 75°<br>2800'×<br>10°14'<br>Traverse to R. 4° | 72°<br>2875'×<br>11°5'<br>Traverse to Right 1° | 73°<br>2775'×<br>10°2'<br>Traverse to Right 1° | 73°×<br>2775'<br>10°2'<br>Traverse to Right 1° |
| F. | | | Guns told off to search beyond E. Barrage | | | | | | | | | |

All Guns will always be ready to fire on Fredericks Barrage lines

# WAR DIARY
## of No 102 M.G. Coy
### INTELLIGENCE SUMMARY
*(Erase heading not required.)*

Vol XIV

Army Form C. 2118.

| Place | Date | Hour | Summary of Events and Information | Remarks and references to Appendices |
|---|---|---|---|---|
| | 1/5/17 | 1 a.m | Remainder of Coy ie B & C Sections relieved by 2 Sections of No 11 M.G. Coy at 2 Dec. The Company bivouaced at Transport lines near CANDLE FACTORY, ST NICHOLAS G.16.b.6.5. Day spent resting. | Reference map sheet 51bNW. |
| | 2/5/17 | 7am | Orders received from 34th Div? that 102 M.G. Coy would come under the orders of Bdr of Divn and not proceed to the Back Area with the 102 (I.S.) Brigade. Lieut McCouper M.C. acting for C.O. conferred with Bde M.G. Officer of Divn at H.23.C.31. |  |
| | | 9 am | Lt Stapleton M.C. & Lt Anderson arr. 2nd Lieut McDean proceeded to reconnoitre and decide upon positions to be taken up for barrage work. |  |
| | | 10 am 12 noon | Morning employed preparing guns for action. |  |
| | | 9 p.m | Coy moved to SUNKEN ROAD running northwards from H.23.d.80.80 to H.23.B.85.10, A Section on left, then B, C & D Sections in succession from the left. Labs and emplacements were made & all arrangements made for opening fire on barrage lines:-
Section 1 end of ROEUX  I.19.C.60.20.
Section 2 end of ROEUX  I.20.C.00.20.  Cents of ROEUX I.20C.00.90.
Section 3 ExLn of ROEUX I.20A.60.30. |  |
| | 3/5/17 |  | Fire opened on these lines from zero hour to zero + 36 mins. Relieved in by Artillery slight during the day; intermittent enemy m.g. fire. |  |

McCouper Lieut
for O.C. 102 M.G. Coy.

Army Form C. 2118.

# WAR DIARY
## —or—
## INTELLIGENCE SUMMARY. of No. 102 M.G. Coy.

Vol XIX

(Erase heading not required.)

Instructions regarding War Diaries and Intelligence Summaries are contained in F.S. Regs., Part II. and the Staff Manual respectively. Title pages will be prepared in manuscript.

| Place | Date | Hour | Summary of Events and Information | Remarks and references to Appendices |
|---|---|---|---|---|
| | 3/5/17 | 10pm | Coy stood by to open fire on S.O.S. line running through Cemetery 1.9.B.35.25. to I.9.d.70.35. S.O.S. message was not sent up. Night was very quiet. | Reference map sheet 57 D N.W. |
| | 4/5/17 | | very little shelling on both sides. Hostile shelling at infrequent intervals during the day. Coy proceeded to transport lines at ST. NICHOLAS and bivouacked for the night. | |
| | 5/5/17 | | Large ammunition dump in ARRAS caught fire and blazed all the night. | |
| | 6/5/17 | | Company entrained at ST. NICHOLAS for BARLY. Joined XVIIth Army Corps. Church Parade. 2nd Lieut J. M. Dixon received special leave from G.O.C. 102 Bgde and proceeds to LE TREPORT to visit wounded brother. | |
| | 7/5/17 | | Route marched to NERGNY. Joined XIXth Army Corps. | |
| | 8/5/17 | | Route marched to BOUQUEMAISON. | |
| AUTHEUX | 9/5/17 | | Route marched to AUTHEUX. | |
| | 10/5/17 | | Lt. C.P.B. Sanger + 2nd Lieut J.C.K. Chase joined the Coy from Base Depot. | |
| | 11/5/17 | | Programme of Training Commenced. | |
| | 13/5/17 | | Swimming Parade, Gas drill + lecture. Church Parade. | |

Rutherford Heron
[?] O.C. 102 M.G.Coy.

# WAR DIARY
## INTELLIGENCE SUMMARY
*(Erase heading not required.)*

of No. 102 M.G. Coy

Army Form C. 2118.

Title pages Vol XIV will be prepared in manuscript.

| Place | Date | Hour | Summary of Events and Information | Remarks and references to Appendices |
|---|---|---|---|---|
| AUTHEUX | 14/3/17 | | A+B Section fires on Range. C+D section's M.G. drill as 2nd Lieut. McKeon upon from Seine leave. | map reference Sheet 51S N.W. |
| | 15/3/17 | | C+D Sections on Range. A+B Sections gun drill &c. Coy inspected at work by G.O.C. 102 (I.S.) Brigade, also transport. | |
| | 16/3/17 | | Training continued:- M.G. Signals indirect fire, gun laying &c. | |
| | 17/3/17 | | A+B Sections on Range. C+D advanced gun drill. | |
| | 18/3/17 | | C+D Section on Range A+B Sections advanced gun drill. | |
| | 19/3/17 | | Tactical scheme on training area. | |
| | | | Corpl Maclin + Pte Mauritt upon from machine gun school. Lieut McCarter + Hope Graham proceeded on M.G. course at M.G. School | |
| | 20/4/17 | | Brigade Church Parade and march past. G.O.C. 102 Bgade 34th Div. | |
| | 21/3/17 | | A+B Sections on range (advancing with auxiliary mounting) C+D Sections overhauling + range firing with Barr & Stroud. | |
| | 22/3/17 | | C+D on Range. A+B remustering &c. | |
| | 23/3/17 | | A+B Sections of part transport inspected by G.O.C. 102 Bgade in training area, and afterwards took part in Brigade tactical scheme. C+D fired on Range. | |

R. Rutherford Lieut.
O.C. 102 Machine Gun Coy.

# WAR DIARY
## or
## INTELLIGENCE SUMMARY.

(Erase heading not required.)

of No 102 M.G. Coy

Army Form C. 2118.

Instructions regarding War Diaries and Intelligence Summaries are contained in F. S. Regs., Part II. and the Staff Manual respectively. Title pages will be prepared in manuscript. Vol XIV

| Place | Date | Hour | Summary of Events and Information | Remarks and references to Appendices |
|---|---|---|---|---|
| Authaux | 23/5/17 | | The Coy held shoots in the afternoon in conjunction with 23rd Bn N.F. (+ hypnotisation) C.D. Section + part transport inspected by Brigade Commander and afterwards took part in Brigade Tactical Scheme | Map reference Sheet - 51 B N.W |
| | 25/5/17 | | Packing, paddling, weel + cleaning up limbers + Steel helmets painted. The Coy has baths at BERNAVILLÉ | |
| | 26/5/17 | | The Company was inspected by G.O.C. 34th Division and afterwards engaged in Brigade Tactical Scheme raiding as on 23rd + 24/5/17. C.D. in morning A.T.B. in afternoon Clin Young A. joined the Coy from 87th M.G. Coy. | |
| | 27/5/17 | | Church Parades | |
| | 28/5/17 | | Loading up limbers &c. | |
| | 29/5/17 | | Limbers transport moves off by Road for ST NICHOLAS. Lieut C.R.B. Sawyer in charge. | |
| | 30/5/17 | 9am | Coy inspected by O.C. Company Company marches to CANDAS STATION and entrained for ARRAS. Detrained at ARRAS and marched to Camp near ST NICHOLAS at C.17.a.central in bivouacs. | |
| | 31/5/17 | | Training under Section Officers. | |

R Rutherford Lieut
O.C. 102 M.G. Coy.

Army Form C. 2118.

102 M.G. Coy.

Vol 14

# WAR DIARY
or
## INTELLIGENCE SUMMARY.
(Erase heading not required.)

| Place | Date | Hour | Summary of Events and Information | Remarks and references to Appendices |
|---|---|---|---|---|
| ST NICHOLAS | 1/6/17 | | Physical training. Baths on River Scarpe. Packing limbers. Sent C/S Sawyer Kenepen to No 171 M.G. Coy as Second in Command. | Ref. Map Sheet. 51.B.N.W. |
| | 2/6/17 | | Lieut H.L. Anderson and 2nd Lieut F.W. Dixon together with section sergeants of A&B Sections, reconnoitred the ground for the advance. A&B Sections went through a practice attack with the Infantry Battalions of the 102 (Tyneside Scottish) Brigade in the evening on the Divisional training ground. | |
| | 3/6/17 | 11 am 12pm | A number of enemy aeroplanes flew over the camp, & dropped about 12 bombs on Roud and St Nicholas. Lieut J. Rutherford (acting O.C. Coy) and 2nd Lieut R.A. Thomas (D Section) and 2 N.C.O. reconnoitred the trenches early morning. D&B Sections (8 guns) relieves 8 guns of No 101 M.G. Coy in position shown on map A. attached on accordance with 102 (T.S.) Brigade orders No 1. For the advance up the Western Slope of Infanchone Hill. Guides from 101 M.G. Coy met A&B Sections at Tank dump at 11 a.c.3. | Pouvoni rested ⑩ on Map |

Rutherford
O.C. 102 M.G. Coy.

# WAR DIARY
## or
## INTELLIGENCE SUMMARY

Army Form C.2...

| Place | Date | Hour | Summary of Events and Information | Remarks and references to Appendices |
|---|---|---|---|---|
| | 3/6/17 | | Two machine guns and teams are allotted to each of the assaulting Battalions for the Consolidation of CHARLIE and CURLY TRENCHES. I.17.d. and I.7.d. Guns and teams are allotted to Battalions as shewn on map. The two guns in CADIZ TRENCH were in Brigade Reserve was at A.12.B. & A.12.d. | Ref map sheet 51b N.W |
| | | 8pm | C & D Sections proceeded to line of trenches H.6.a.4.1. to H.6.c.15.70. and proceeded to dig emplacements for guns during the barrage work during the advance up the western slope of greenland hill. by 102 (T.S.) Brigade. | |
| | | 11pm 12midnight | Enemy aircraft again active bomb dropping over ARRAS and immediate district. | |
| | 4 | 9pm | No 83038 L/Corporal Guerra and No 33740 Pte Taylor H. wounded by shell fire. O.C. Coy Capt. and C-O Rectord moved to position in TELFORD TRENCH H.6.a.9.0. Rations and stores all in position by 11.30 p.m. During the night work was carried out on emplacements by C & D Sections to render them fit for firing. | |

Rothwell A
O.C. 102 M.G. Coy.

# WAR DIARY
## of
## INTELLIGENCE SUMMARY.
(Erase heading not required.)

Army Form C. 2118.

| Place | Date | Hour | Summary of Events and Information | Remarks and references to Appendices |
|---|---|---|---|---|
| | 5/6/17 | | Intermittent shelling during the morning and afternoon. No material damage done | Ref map Sheet 51b NW |
| | | 10 am | 2nd Lieut McDiven should all correct in front line. Situation quiet and no casualties. Lieut Anderson reports A section O.K. | |
| | | 4 pm | From O.C.M.G.C. (Major Kelleby) makes barrage positions and gave final instructions: | |
| | | 8 pm | The eight guns of C.D. sections opened out according to programme and fired until 8.30 pm. In all 1800 rounds fired. The stoppages which occurred were due chiefly to faulty ammunition & hourly to faulty check lever. | |
| | | 9 pm | Objectives taken by Infantry; hostile retaliation appeared weak and uncertain. His shells fell near gun positions. Casualties nil. | |
| | | 10 pm | D.M.G.O reports that all objectives taken. CHARLIE & CURLY TRENCHES held throughout their length and CUTHBERT & COD held by posts strong posts being established as per programme at junction of CUTHBERT & H. |  |

Rutherford.
O.C. 102 M.G. Coy.

# WAR DIARY
## or
## INTELLIGENCE SUMMARY.
*(Erase heading not required.)*

Army Form C. 2118.

| Place | Date | Hour | Summary of Events and Information | Remarks and references to Appendices |
|---|---|---|---|---|
| | 5/6/17 | | and CHARLIE and SALUTE pushed out along trench running NE. | Ref Maps Sheets 51² N.W |
| | | 9h | Division on right have made satisfactory progress also. The night of the 5/6th passed quietly so far as our own Division in TELFORD TRENCH were concerned but there was considerable activity on part of enemy on our front line wiring and digging parties of 26th N.F. suffered heavy casualties. | |
| | | 11.30 pm | Message received to say that a fighting patrol of R.F.C. would be over our lines at 3.45 am b/f if to locate possible massing of enemy troops preparatory to counter attack. The signal from aeroplane was to be white light, red light, white light. Our machine guns were to open fire on protective barrage line immediately the signal was observed. The signal was not sent. Lieut Col. Anderson reported the two guns with 22/19 N.F. in position in strong point near junction of CHARLIE and CURLY TRENCHES. Remaining 2 guns of Allerton in position in front of 21/19 N.F. | |

Plowright
OC 105 M.G. Coy

# WAR DIARY
## or
## INTELLIGENCE SUMMARY.
(Erase heading not required.)

Army Form C. 2118.

Instructions regarding War Diaries and Intelligence Summaries are contained in F.S. Regs, Part II. and the Staff Manual respectively. Title pages Vol XV will be prepared in manuscript.

| Place | Date | Hour | Summary of Events and Information | Remarks and references to Appendices |
|---|---|---|---|---|
| | 5/6/17 | | 2nd Lieut McDuff (6 Section) informs that from 8 pm onwards CADIZ TRENCH was heavily shelled, and that B Section gun teams not yet moved forward and awaiting orders. | Ref map sheet 57 D NW |
| | 6/6/17 | 6 pm | as CURLY TRENCH not yet in our hands. Message received that guns had to be ready to open fire on barrage line if required. | |
| | | 10.45 | One gun team of B Section buried by shell, and all gun team (wounded) except the N.C.O.'s who dug the team out. Gun withdrawn to be cleaned examined. | |
| | | 10 pm | At 10 pm S.O.S. signal was observed on our front when the eight guns of C Section immediately opened fire on S.O.S. line and maintained a rapid concentrated fire until 10.30 pm when fire was gradually slackened down to a ceasefire at 11.30 pm | |
| | | 12 midnight | The S.O.S. signal again went up. Fire was again opened and our S.O.S. barrage line was maintained up till 12.45 am | |

J Hartley Lt
O.C. 102 M.G. Coy

**Army Form C. 2118.**

# WAR DIARY
## or
## INTELLIGENCE SUMMARY.
*(Erase heading not required.)*

Vol XV

Instructions regarding War Diaries and Intelligence Summaries are contained in F.S. Regs., Part II. and the Staff Manual respectively. Title pages will be prepared in manuscript.

| Place | Date | Hour | Summary of Events and Information | Remarks and references to Appendices |
|---|---|---|---|---|
| | 7/6/17 | 12.45 a.m. | Some number of Rounds expended during both shoots 50,000. Rounds for the night guns. There was no shooting near gun positions. Remainder of night passed quietly. | Refer to Sheet 57B NW. |
| | 8/6/17 | | The night of the 7/8th passed quietly, as far as our gun positions were concerned. | |
| | 9/6/17 | | The eight forward guns of A & B Sections were relieved on night of 8/9 by 8 guns of No. 101 M.G. Coy. On relief A+B Sections took (late 4th Anderson + type) brigade Transport on Course at M.G. School in accordance with 102 Brigade Instructions (by withdrawing from line and | |
| | 9/6/17 | | returned to Camp at SAINT NICHOLAS. on night of 9/10. Pvt 87608pr (2nd in Command) who was on Course at Machine Gun School was admitted to Hospital at ETAPLES and evacuated to England sick. | |
| ST. NICHOLAS | 10/6/17 | | Day spent resting and cleaning up. | |
| " | 11/6/17 | | Coy. bathed at Pardonne Baths. | |
| " | 12/6/17 | | Inspection of Box Anti Gas apparatus. Boy relieved no. 103 Machine Gun Coy on the night of 12/13 in the left ¼ ilion 34th Division front. | |

J. Huntley Lt.
O.C. 102. M.G. Coy.

**WAR DIARY**
or
**INTELLIGENCE SUMMARY.**

Army Form C. 2118.

Vol XV

| Place | Date | Hour | Summary of Events and Information | Remarks and references to Appendices |
|---|---|---|---|---|
| | 13/6/17 | | Gun positions taken over are as under:— | Ref map sheet 57BNW |
| | | | No 1. I.11.b.3.6. — No 2. I.11.b.1.8. CONRAD TRENCH |  |
| | | | No 3. I.11.b.1.5. No 4. I.1.c.8.3. CORK TRENCH |  |
| | | | CHILI TRENCH. |  |
| | | | No 5. H.12.B.45.75. |  |
| | | | No 6. M.6.c.5.5. |  |
| | | | No 7. H.6.c.55. — HAWTHORNE TRENCH about 50x apart. |  |
| | | | No 8. H.6.a.4.1. — Entrance to CIVIL TRENCH |  |
| | | | No 9. H.11.b.9.6. } Hilly trench at 50 yards intervals |  |
| | | | " 10 to |  |
| | | | " 11 H.12.a.2.8. |  |
| | | | " 12 |  |
| | | | Guns at H.6.a.4.1. and 1 gun in Hilly trench used as Anti-Aircraft Guns, and Hille Jackson sights were taken over at these positions. |  |
| | | | One section of 102 M.G. Coy relieved one section of 103 M.G. Coy in Reserve in Railway Cutting H.14.a. |  |
| | | | All reliefs completed by 1 am 13/6/17. |  |
| | | 8pm | A hostile aeroplane flew over our lines at 8pm. When it went immediately engaged by both our Anti aircraft machine guns. It then turned over our lines and was engaged by one of our aeroplanes. |  |

J Rathof Lieut

O.C. 102 M.G. Coy

# WAR DIARY
## or
## INTELLIGENCE SUMMARY.

Army Form C. 2118.

| Place | Date | Hour | Summary of Events and Information | Remarks and references to Appendices |
|---|---|---|---|---|
| | 13/6/17 | | An intermittent fire was maintained by two of our guns in HOLLY TRENCH from 10.30 p.m. 13/6/17 to 1 a.m. 14/6/17. Last intended during the day 2000 Rounds | Ref Maps Sheet 57B NW |
| | 14/6/17 | | Work was carried out in CORK TRENCH, T.1.a.7+ in accordance with OMGO's Instruction. Day passed quietly, very little shelling near gun positions except the gun in CORK TRENCH at T.1.a.83. which was heavily shelled from 9 a.m. - 3 p.m. Hostile aircraft were active flying low over our lines at 9.15 a.m. and 4.5 p.m. and were engaged by our two anti aircraft machine guns when they turned back over their own lines. Work was done in improving the trenches in the vicinity of gun positions. | |
| | 15/6/17 | | Hostile aircraft again active flying low over our trenches. Fire was opened on enemy aeroplanes at 7.30 p.m. + 8 p.m. and maintained till same retired. | |

Sud
[signature]
O.C. 102 M.G. Coy

# WAR DIARY
## or
## INTELLIGENCE SUMMARY.
(Erase heading not required)

Army Form C. 2118.

Vol XV

| Place | Date | Hour | Summary of Events and Information | Remarks and references to Appendices |
|---|---|---|---|---|
| | 16/9/17 | 2am to 7.30am | All gun positions heavily shelled, HOLLY TRENCH where all aircraft gun crew were receiving considerable attention. Hostile aeroplanes appeared low over our trenches but relied on being engaged by our anti-aircraft machine guns. Cuba and Bank Trenches were reconnoitred with a view to selecting m.g. emplacements and dugout. Position selected in Cork Trench at 1.10.2.2.3. Lieut Aretwith joined the Coy. and posted to C.Section. | Ref Map Sheet 5-1-2 N.W. |
| | 16/9/17 | 7.9 pm | Hostile activity below normal. Hostile aeroplane over our trenches and engaged by our a.a. machine guns when it turned back. Work was carried out on HUSSAR and HOLLY TRENCHES deepening and deepening in Cuba holes, CORK TRENCH was deepened and widened. For war August at I.7.a.62.23. The section in reserve relieved Section in front system. | |
| | 16/9/17 | | Capt J.R. Pyper M.C. joined Coy from Base Depot. | |

[signatures]
OC 103 M.G. Coy

# WAR DIARY
## or
## INTELLIGENCE SUMMARY.
(Erase heading not required.)

Army Form C. 2118.

Instructions regarding War Diaries and Intelligence Summaries are contained in F.S. Regs., Part II. and the Staff Manual respectively. Title pages Vol XV will be prepared in manuscript.

| Place | Date | Hour | Summary of Events and Information | Remarks and references to Appendices |
|---|---|---|---|---|
| | 12/6/17 | 7k. | Enemy put down Barrage on road in front of GAVRELLE LINE. No damage was done. 2nd 4.2 shell fell in vicinity of HOLLY TRENCH. The trench junction C.VIII, HELFORD and HOOD was shelled intermittently throughout the night. Heavies ones of our machine guns at the front H.6. a.1.1. | Reference Sheet 51B N.W. |
| | | 10pm | Signaling with a red lamp was observed in the direction of VITRY, but no message was made out. Went was carried out in improving HUSSAR TRENCH and recommitted of new augout in COPSE TRENCH the given. | |
| | 13/6/17 | 4.50 am | Hostile aeroplane flew low over our trenches but within Richards out of range when a.a. machine gun opened fire. | |
| | 13/6/17 | | The junction of CALEDONIAN TRENCH and the GAVRELLE line were heavily shelled during the night of 12/9/13. Hostile aircraft was again active over our trenches during the day, but out of range of our a.a. machine guns. | |

Rottwell Lieut
O.C. 102 M.G. Coy

Army Form C. 2118.

# WAR DIARY
## or
## INTELLIGENCE SUMMARY.
(Erase heading not required.)

Vol XV

Instructions regarding War Diaries and Intelligence Summaries are contained in F. S. Regs., Part II. and the Staff Manual respectively. Title pages will be prepared in manuscript.

| Place | Date | Hour | Summary of Events and Information | Remarks and references to Appendices |
|---|---|---|---|---|
| | 19/6/17 | 5.30 a.m. | Enemy aeroplane observed flying low over own trenches. M.G. fire was opened on it when it was seen but it appeared after a few minutes and fire was again opened on it. The plane then flew away over its own lines as though hit. Work was carried out on improvements on trenches in vicinity of pontoons and excavation of chalks for new dugouts in CORK TRENCH. Hostile artillery active during the night of 19/4/20/6 on HOLLY TRENCH and scored direct hits obtained on Bell bomb emplacement and one emplacement damaged. The gun was moved to a position of one emplacement damaged. The gun near junction of CIVIL, HELFORD and HOOD TRENCHES was moved to a position 20 yards along HELFORD TRENCH on account of heavy shelling. Work was continued on the dugouts in CORK TRENCH and improving & remodelling around the positions. | Ref. Trench Maps Sheet 51b N.W. |
| | 20/6/17 | | The day was utilised in the line by no. 50 m.g. Coy. and returned to Camp at St NICOLAS on the night of 20/21/6. | |
| | 21/6/17 | | Embussed at the OCTROI, ARRAS for BUNEVILLE. arriving 3.30 pm. | |

Rutherford Capt /M

**Army Form C. 2118.**

# WAR DIARY
## or
## INTELLIGENCE SUMMARY.

(Erase heading not required.)

Vol 1

| Place | Date | Hour | Summary of Events and Information | Remarks and references to Appendices |
|---|---|---|---|---|
| BUNEVILLE | 27/6/17 | 10.0 a.m. | Coy paraded for Inspection by O.C. Coy. | |
| | 23/6/17 | | Squad drill v. O.C's parade, and packing of limbers. | |
| | 24/6/17 | | Church parade. | |
| | 25/6/17 to 30/6/17 | | Training carried out as per programme of training attached and marked appendix | |
| | 29/6/17 | | 2nd Lieuts. B.E. Drew and F.B. Dowson joined the Coy from Base Depot | |
| | 30/6/17 | | Company Sports. | |

J.R. Ruttle
Lieut Col.
O.C. 102. M.G. Coy.

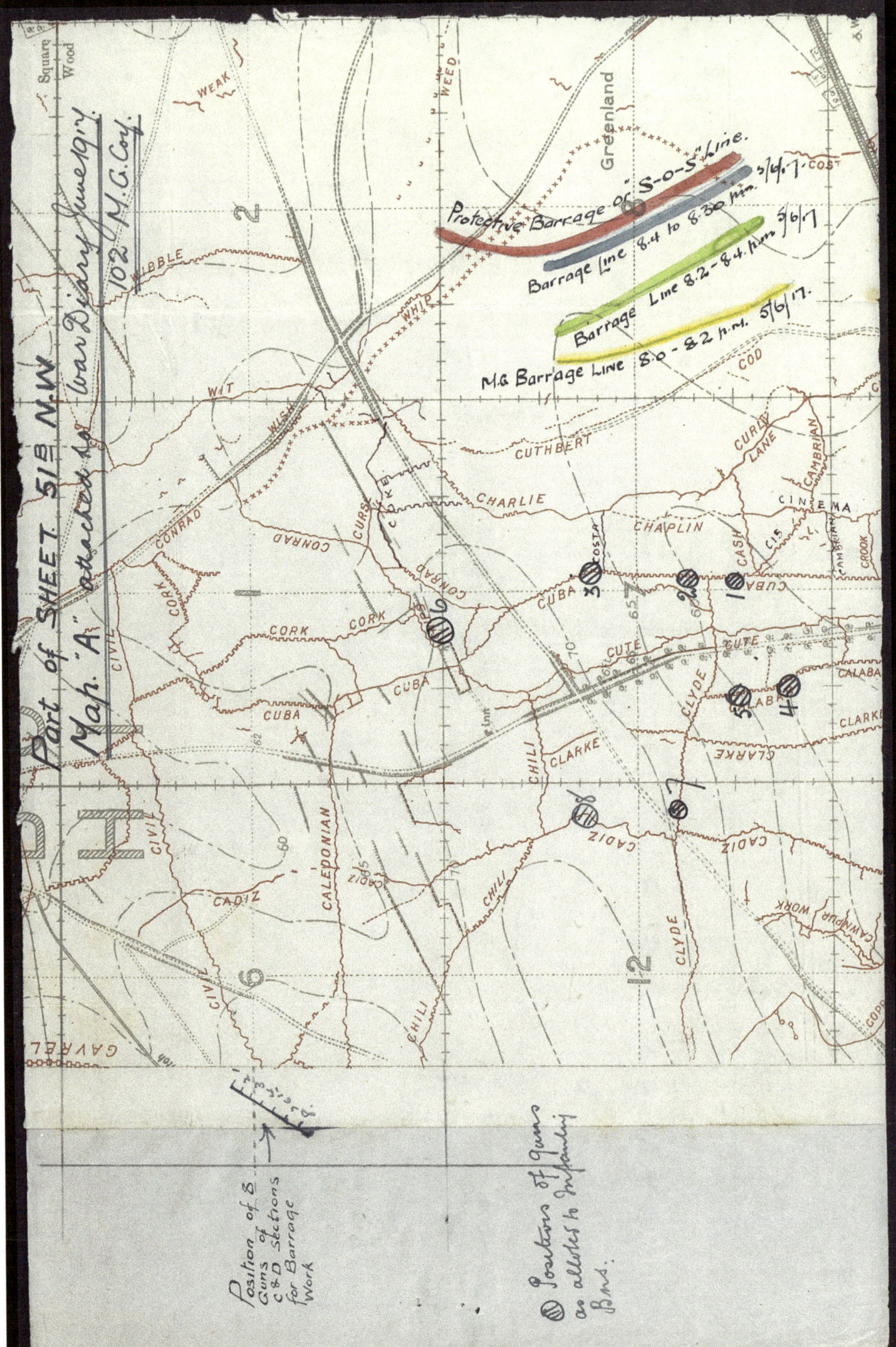

Appendix B.
War Diary
June 1917

# PROGRAMME of FIRE FOR Nº 4. GUN.

Laying to be checked every 100 Rounds

From Zero hour to Zero + 2 minutes.
  To Barrage Nº 1 Target.
  Bearing         131° Mag.
  Angle of Quadrant Elevation.   6° 48'
  Rate of Fire ----------- MAXIMUM.
  Traverse to..... 132° 30'.

From Zero + 2 mins to Zero + 4 mins.
  To Barrage Nº 2 Target.
  Bearing      129° Mag.
  Angle of Quadrant Elevation.   7° 34'
  Rate of Fire ----------- MAXIMUM
  Traverse to right 130° 30'.

From Zero + 4 mins to Zero + 30 mins:-
  To Barrage Nº 3 Target
  Bearing    127° Mag.
  Angle of Quadrant Elevation   8° 15'
  Rate of Fire ------- Maximum to Zero + 20 mins
                       When fire will be gradually
                       slackened to a cease fire at Zero + 30 mins
  Traverse to... 128° 30'.

At Zero + 30 mins:
  Lay on the protective Barrage or "S-O-S" line
  Bearing   123° Mag.
  Angle of Quadrant Elevation.   7° 15'
  Traverse to right 2 degrees.

                    J. Rutherford  Lieut
                    O.C 102 m.g. Coy.

# Instructions re Barrage Guns.

Appendix "C" War Diary June 17

I. The Guns of C Section will be called "A" Group, and the Guns of D Section D Group. Guns will be numbered 1 to 8 from the right.

II. During the whole of Z day, either an Officer or a Senior N.C.O. will be in charge of each group of Guns.

III. Two men will be on duty at all times with each Gun. One of these men's sole duty will be to look out for signals (e.g. the "S.O.S") which may be sent up by the Infantry. The other man must be a capable number one.

IV. Every precaution must be taken that neither the Gun nor the Gun numbers, are visible to the enemy even at long ranges.

V. Auxiliary aiming marks will be placed for each Gun in order to check any slight movement of the Tripod.

Zero line for each Gun will be 90° magnetic.

VI. After the "Cease fire" at Zero + 30 minutes not more than 1 Gun in any group will be taken out of action at any time for any purpose whatever.

VII. After Zero + 30 mins: guns will be employed on a protective barrage, (i.e. the "S-O-S" line) Guns will be ready to fire on this line <u>immediately</u>. Guns will be kept <u>half loaded</u>.

VIII. Two petrol tins of water must be kept near the Emplacement.

J. Rutherford Lieut
O.C. 102 M.G. Coy.

4/6/17

Orders for Gun Numbers &c.

Appendix C.
(War Diary)
June 1917

I. One man will always be on duty to keep a strict lookout for signals (such as the "S.O.S.") which may be sent up by the Infantry.

II. A capable number one will also always be on duty at the Gun.

III. The Gun will be kept half loaded.

IV. There must be as little movement as possible near the Gun and every precaution must be taken that neither the Gun nor the Gun Team is observed by the enemy even at long ranges.

V. S.O.S. signal will be two RED Rockets or Very Lights fired in rapid succession.

8th June 1917.

J Rutherford Lieut
O.C. 102 M.G. Coy

Appendix "D"
War Diary

Programme of Training for week ending 30/6/17
102 M.G. Coy.

| Date | Hours | Nature of Training | Locality | Remarks |
|---|---|---|---|---|
| June 25th | 6.45 – 7.30 a.m.<br>9.0 – 9.50 "<br>10.0 – 10.50 "<br>11.0 – 11.50 "<br>12.0 – 12.50 p.m.<br>2.30 – 4.0 " | Parade under C.S.M. Squad drill & Saluting.<br>Physical Training.<br>Care & Cleaning – Shore parks.<br>Gun Drill.<br>Company Drill<br>Recreational Training | Training Ground. | Lecture for Junior N.C.O's<br>5-6 p.m |
| 26th | | As for 25th | — " — | N.C.O's Class<br>5-6 p.m |
| 27th | 6.45 – 7.30 a.m.<br>9.00 a.m – 1 p.m.<br>2.30 – 4 p.m. | Parade under C.S.M. Squad drill & Saluting<br>Route March, Tactical Schemes<br>Recreational Training | Buneville – A.10.c.<br>– Cross Road A.11.b. central<br>– Buneville<br>Training Ground. | — " — |
| 28th | 6.45 – 7.30 a.m.<br>9.0 am – 1.0 p.m.<br>9.0 – 9.50 am<br>10.0 – 10.50 "<br>11.0 – 11.50 "<br>12.0 – 12.50 p.m. | Parade under C.S.M.<br>A.&B. on Range.<br>C & D. Physical training<br>— " — Gas Drill<br>— " — Gun Drill<br>— " — I.A. | Training Ground.<br>Range G.5.a. 2.9.<br>Training Ground | Recreational training 2.30 – 4.0 p.m. |
| 29th | | As for 28th but C & D on Range | | N.C.O's Class. 5-6 p.m.<br>— " — |
| 30th | 6.45 – 7.30 a.m.<br>9.0 – 9.50 "<br>10.0 – 11.50<br>12.0 – 12.50 p.m.<br>2.0 – 4.0 p.m. | Parade under C.S.M.<br>Physical Training<br>Tests of Elementary Training.<br>Coy. Drill<br>Recreational Training | Training Ground | |

23 – 6 – 17.

[signature]
O.C. 102 M.G. Coy.

# WAR DIARY

## INTELLIGENCE SUMMARY

of 102 M.G. Coy.

Vol XVI

Army Form C. 2118.

| Place | Date | Hour | Summary of Events and Information | Remarks and references to Appendices |
|---|---|---|---|---|
| BUNEVILLE | 1/7/17 | | Brigade Church parades, and "March past" at Monts-au-Terroil. | |
| | 2/7/17 | | Usual training parades, also Gas demonstration by Divisional Anti Gas Officer. | Ref. Map Sheet. |
| | 3/7/17 | | Party of 9 O.R. & 1 Sergt. represented the Coy at Divisional medal distribution. Packing lunches &c. Orders received that 34th Divisional was to be transferred from 17th Corps to 31st Corps and that 102 M.G. Coy would move to ROISELLE AREA on night of 4th/5th/7/17 and would be temporarily attached to Cavalry Corps while in Cavalry Corps Area. | 52 C NE |
| | 4/7/17 | | Coy and transport marched to TINCQUES and entrained. | |
| | 5/7/17 | 3.30 am | Arrived PERONNE STATION and detrained. Marched to HAMELET. Coy billeted in Huts. | |
| HAMELET | 6/7/17 | 9.30am 11.30 2pm | Preparing guns and equipment for the trenches. Particularly packing preliminary M.O's a/c on the lecture by Lieut. R.S. Anderson on "new barrage methods". | |
| " | 7/7/17 | 9.0am | Range firing Class and anti Gas lecture. Practicing concealment of guns and coming into action. | |

R.S. Anderson Lieut for
O.C. 102 M.G. Coy.

# WAR DIARY
## INTELLIGENCE SUMMARY

Vol XVI  102 M.G. Coy.

Army Form C. 2118.

| Place | Date | Hour | Summary of Events and Information | Remarks and references to Appendices |
|---|---|---|---|---|
| HAMELET | 2/2/17 | 8 p.m. | An advance body from D section and 2 guns of C Section (consisting of 2 men per gun team) proceeded to the line, near Pont Ytteinberg, to B2 Subsector, 34th Division front, to be attached to the respective positions their guns were take over. | Ref map 62 C N.E. |
|  | 2/2/17 | 7.45 p.m. | Gun teams of D section and 2 teams of C Section under 2nd Lt. R.J. Thomas marched off to the trenches and relieved guns of the 4th Cavalry M.G. Squadron in B2 Subsector 34th Divn. front. | |
|  |  |  | An advance body of 2 men per gun team from A+B sections and remaining 2 teams of C Section proceeded near 2nd Lieut? B.A. Terry & Sutherden and were attached to the respective positions they were retaking in B1 + B3 Subsector, 34th Division front. | |
|  | 2/2/17 |  | A + B Sections and 2 teams of C Section relieved guns of 4th Cavalry M.G. Squadron in B1. + B3 Subsectors, 34th Divn. Front. Positions of all M.G.s were as follows:— No. 2 Position L.22.d.16.  No.4 — L.22 c.4.4. No.6 — L.22 a.10.10. No.7, L.22 c.90.90. No.9. L.17 d.6.9.7.   No.10A L.11.a.95.70.  No.12, L.17a oo.77.  No.14 L.16 c 45.05. No.17 L.10d 2.4.   No.19 - L.10 b.4.0.  No.21. L.11 b.o.8.  21A L.11 b. 05.38. No.24 L.5 c 4.6.  No.25 - L.10.b.  No.36.  L.10.b.4.6. No.22, L.5 d 65.55. Corps Supersessions COTE WOOD L.10.C.3.2 R.B. Anderson, Major, M.G. Coy. O.C. 102 M.G. Coy. | |

# WAR DIARY

102 M.G. Coy.

## INTELLIGENCE SUMMARY. Vol. XVI.

Army Form C. 2118.

| Place | Date | Hour | Summary of Events and Information | Remarks and references to Appendices |
|---|---|---|---|---|
| | 9/7/17 | | During the night of 9th/10th there was a slight increase of hostile artillery activity but no shelling near our gun positions. No firing carried out by us. Chauderie nil. Work in B2 subsector continued in improving positions. | Ref. Map Sheet 62c NE |
| | 10/7/17 5.? | 6 a.m. | Hostile artillery continues very active. VILLERET. HARGICOURT and left of No.22 position were shelled by 77 cm and trench mortars. 50% being blind. | |
| | 11/7/17 | 6 a.m. | 17-77mm shells fell to the west of COTE WOOD (sq. K2) during the night. Enemy machine guns were active during the night. Reserve of SAA at gun positions complete and local improvements to trenches carried out. No firing carried out. Chauderie nil. | |
| | 11/7/17 to 12/7/17 | 6 a.m. | Enemy artillery again active. INDIAN + SEC TRENCHES, The Valley in front of THE CHATEAU and THE LE VERGUIER ROAD and HARGICOURT were shelled intermittently. VILLERET was shelled continuously with 77cm + 10.5cm shells also French Mortars. 50% of the 10.5cm shells were blind. Enemy m.g's too active than usual. Two m.g.s were located firing from approximately G.20. Central + G.7.a.7.4. were very lightly When were late up by enemy. Two green lights were sent up. GRAND PRIEL FARM. No apparent action followed. Drawing rifle and bombing cards. Lieut. Smith wounded slightly and continues to keep audience. Lieut. Hudson took over duties of Lieutenant offices on relief from leave. | |

H.S. Anderson
O.C. 102 M.G. Coy.

# WAR DIARY or INTELLIGENCE SUMMARY

Army Form C. 2118.

of 102 M.G. Coy.

Vol XVI

| Place | Date | Hour | Summary of Events and Information | Remarks and references to Appendices |
|---|---|---|---|---|
| | 12/7/17 to 13/7/17 | 6 a.m. | Our m.g. position at L.17.b.9.7. was lightly shelled on 12th. in enemy zone. The two hostile m.g.'s previously reported firing from G.20. central and G.7.a.9.4. fired at CHATEAU and theory, commencing 9.30 p.m. We replied to the fire of these guns which ceased fire for 3/4 hour after our retaliation, and subsequent shoots were promptly replied to by our guns and their rate of fire decreased considerably. | Ref map. Sheet 52c NE |
| | 13/7/17 to 14/7/17 | 6 a.m. | VILLERET was shelled from 8.20 a.m. to 9.15 a.m. 13th. At 11.10 pm 13th. enemy artillery of all calibres opened fairly rapid fire on forward posts of B.1 Subsector. Rate of fire decreased at 11.30 p.m. and ceased 11.40 pm, but was renewed at 2.0 am 14th. and west of the Subsector was systematically shelled with 77—, 4.2"—, 5.9"— minenwerfer, a number of gas shells were used. At 2.25 am enemy attacked UNNAMED FARM and INDIAN TRENCH and succeeded in entering INDIAN trench and capturing 6 men and a Lewis gun. At 2.30 am S.O.S. signal was observed in B.2 Subsector. On our No. 10 gun opening fire it was immediately bombarded with 15 minenwerfer and had to be transferred to another position. Enemy m.g. at G.14.c.5.7. opened fire as usual at 9.15 pm 13th. We answered replied with m.g. fire and at 10 p.m. enemy guns ceased fire. Hostile m.g. firing from G.13.b.25.25. was silenced by our m.g. retaliation. Hostile aeroplane when at our lines at 4.20 pm 13th. was engaged by our anti aircraft machine guns when it returned to investigate. |  |

M.G. Anderson
O.C. 102 M.G. Coy 2nd Lt

Army Form C. 2118.

# WAR DIARY
## or
## INTELLIGENCE SUMMARY of 102 M.G. Coy.
### Vol XVI
(Erase heading not required.)

Instructions regarding War Diaries and Intelligence Summaries are contained in F.S. Regs., Part II. and the Staff Manual respectively. Title pages will be prepared in manuscript.

| Place | Date | Hour | Summary of Events and Information | Remarks and references to Appendices |
|---|---|---|---|---|
| | 13/7/17 to 14/7/17 | 6 a.m. | Anti-aircraft lookin built at no. 17 position. and one improved at no. 17 position, also improvements of trenches and emplacements carried out. | Ref: map Sheet 62C NE |
| | 14/7/17 to 15/7/17 | 6 a.m. | Hostile artillery active on usual targets. Its cross roads nr. no 10 position was also shelled by light-movements at 8.45 am 13th. Hostile m.g. appeared to be shifts a little to its left. We kept an intermittent m.g. fire on these guns from 9.15 pm to 12.30 am 15th during which period hostile gun only fired 3 short bursts. | |
| | 15/7/17 to 16/7/17 | 6 a.m. | The usual targets in front line system were active. Three by enemy, of which three appears to be a large number of shrap. Bloss Wood was shelled by all calibres up to 5·9" from 11.40 am to 5.30 pm 15th about 200 shells. – no material damage done. During 16th this shelling our B4 Seebach H.Q. was moved to L.16.d.15.10. Enemy m.g. was less active than usual during the night. Wo. Jervis w/g.s. carried out by us. Pont: Pte Smith of ones Coy. from hospital. | |

R.G. Anderson Lieut for
O.C. 102 M.G. Coy.

Army Form C. 2118.

# WAR DIARY
## INTELLIGENCE SUMMARY. 102 M.G.C.

Vol XVI

(Erase heading not required.)

Instructions regarding War Diaries and Intelligence Summaries are contained in F.S. Regs., Part II. and the Staff Manual respectively. Title pages will be prepared in manuscript.

| Place | Date | Hour | Summary of Events and Information | Remarks and references to Appendices |
|---|---|---|---|---|
| | 16/9/17 to 17/9/17 | 6 a.m. to 6 a.m. | Concentration machine gun fire was carried out by no unit. 8 guns in the following targets commencing at 2.0 a.m. 17th on front target and continued at short intervals 2.45 a.m. 17th; viz:- COLOGNE FARM & approaches, POND COPSE, RUISY FARM, MALAKOFF FARM, COLOGNE SUPPORT TRENCH. Roads & tracks in G/3.b. 7000 Rounds S.A.A. was expended during this shoot. There was no enemy artillery retaliation. VILLERET was shelled with 77mm shells at 8 a.m. & 3 p.m. 16th and also with Howitzers at 3 a.m. 17th. A few 77mm shells fell to the right of KAFFIR COPSE at 1.15 a.m. 17th. | Ref map Sheet 62C N.E. |
| | 17/9/17 to 18/9/17 | 6 a.m. to 6 a.m. | Hostile artillery fairly quiet. Enemy Trench Mortars active against VILLERET. Shells at B1 Subsecs H.Q. L.16.d.15.10. Entrances and sunken road against guns of D section in positions L.10.a.2.4. and L.10.b.4.0. relieves guns of C section in positions L.17.b.9.7. and L.11.d.75.70. | |
| | 18/9/17 to 19/9/17 | 6 a.m. to 6 a.m. | Between 11.30 p.m. 18th & 12.30 a.m. 19th we carried out a machine gun shoot in co-operation with artillery on tracks east of MALAKOFF FARM. The 3 guns at L.11.d.20.40. L.+5.10.60. L.10.b.4.0. were employed. 9000 Rounds S.A.A. were expended. | |

H.C. Anderson Lt
O.C. 102 M.G. Coy.

# WAR DIARY

## INTELLIGENCE SUMMARY of 102 M.G. Coy.

Vol. XVI

Army Form C. 2118.

| Place | Date | Hour | Summary of Events and Information | Remarks and references to Appendices |
|---|---|---|---|---|
| 16.7.17 | 18.7.17<br>19.7.17 | 6 am<br>6 am | 1 Gun also fired 250 rounds from L.22.b.9.7 at Trenches G.14.c.<br>Enemy artillery fairly quiet. Usual intermittent shelling of front-system. | Refer to sheet-<br>52C NE |
|  | 19.7.17<br>to<br>20.7.17 | 6am<br>6am | The eastern side of VILLERET was heavily shelled fairly heavily 9.45 pm. to 11.15 pm 19/6. At 2.30 am heavy fire down in a barrage on VILLERET Road. At 2.50 am 20th this barrage was very heavy but no infantry attack developed. Guns no 22 Gun opened fire on S.O.S. line and kept up fire till the barrage ceased, in reply to our S.O.S. signal 3 of our guns opened fire on UNNAMED FARM, COLOGNE FARM and approaches. 6000 Rounds SAA expended. Two lines of about 10 explosions were heard east of VILLERET at 11.45 pm 19th apparently about 3 miles away. A fire was observed burning in the direction of ST. QUENTIN at 11.30 pm. 19th. |  |
|  | 20.7.17<br>to<br>21.7.17 | 6am<br>6am | Between 11.5 pm 20th + 2.0 am 21st we carried out machine gun fire on the following targets<br>(1) Road from behind COLOGNE FARM through G.1.d, G.2.c+d, G.3.c.<br>1 gun (at L.4.6. 10.60) employed. SAA expended 2500 Rounds. |  |

H.S. Anderson Lieut
oc 102 M.G. Coy.

Army Form C. 2118.

# WAR DIARY
## INTELLIGENCE SUMMARY of 102 M.G.Coy.

Vol XVI

(Erase heading not required.)

| Place | Date | Hour | Summary of Events and Information | Remarks and references to Appendices |
|---|---|---|---|---|
| | 20-7-17 to 21-7-17 | 6 am | M.G. Shoot contd:- <br> (2) Track from G.1.a.5.3 to G.2.a.5.0 and Trails from F.8.a.0.2 to G.8.b.5.8. Guns employed 2 (at L.10.d.15.95 & L.M.C.2.8.) Rounds expended 5250. <br> (3) Road, Tramway and ground East of QUARRY WOOD. 1 Gun employed (at L.16.a.73.75.) Rounds expended. <br> Owing to the above shoot a man of the 3rd German M.G. Coy. lost his way and wandered into our lines and was taken prisoner. Enemy artillery before normal, usual intermittent shelling of forts. | |
| | 21-7-17 to 22-7-17 | 6 am | Demonstrations of our Sol. Signal (Rifle Grenade bursting into 2 red 2 white stars) was given between 10 pm & 11 pm 21/7. Enemy then opened out with artillery and trench mortars from 10.10 pm to 10.30 pm on SLAG TRENCH to the EGG and grounds behind. N.B.) Slight bursting Shrapnel & Trench Mortar gas bombs were used. The gas bombardment was repeated between 11.15 pm & 11.40 pm 21/5. The gas had a not unpleasant sweet smelling musk. None of our gunners were effected. Men who were "gassed" were totally unable to walk. The box respirator was found to give complete protection. Hostile m.gs very active at "stands" evening & morning | |

R.G. Anderson
O.C. 102 M.G. Coy.

# WAR DIARY

## INTELLIGENCE SUMMARY

of 102 M.G.C.

Vol LXVI

Army Form C. 2118.

| Place | Date | Hour | Summary of Events and Information | Remarks and references to Appendices |
|---|---|---|---|---|
| | 22-7-7 | 6 a.m. | Usual enemy artillery activity against the SLAG HEAP and MARCOURT. Rifle grenades | Ref was Sheet 62CNE |
| | 23-7-7 | 6 a.m. | were used against our M.G. posts during the 22nd but no damage done. Enemy aircraft very active and engaged by our anti-aircraft machine guns. The night was quiet except for usual enemy M.Gs. at Manchils evening and morning. | |
| | 23-7-7 | 6 a.m. | SLAG TRENCH was L.5. & was shelled with 10.5 cm and 15 cm shells and T.M. gas bombs between 10.45 p.m. and 11.15 p.m. A number of rifle grenades were used against | |
| | 24-7-7 | 6 a.m. | No. 22 position. Improvements to trenches and emplacements carried out at nos. 4, 6, 21 & 23 positions. A leg fire was observed burning throughout day and night in ST. QUENTIN. | |

R.S. Anderson
O.C. 102 M.G. Coy. Lt Col

**WAR DIARY**
OF 102 M.G. Coy

**INTELLIGENCE SUMMARY.**

Vol XVI

Army Form C. 2118.

| Place | Date | Hour | Summary of Events and Information | Remarks and references to Appendices |
|---|---|---|---|---|
| | 24/7-17 | 6 am | We carried out machine gun fire from 11.0 pm 24th to 1.50 a.m. 25th on the following targets:- | Reference |
| | 25.7.17 | 6 am | (1) Road north of MALAKOFF FARM: Guns employed 1. (at L.10.b.4.6.) S.A.A. expended 2,300 Rds. | Sheet 62CNE |
| | | | (2) Rocks behind MALAKOFF FARM. Guns employed 2. (at L.11.c.1.8 & L.17.b.3.6) S.A.A expended. 5,750 Rds. | |
| | | | (3) SUGAR TRENCH. Guns employed 1. (at L.17.6.3.6) S.A.A expended 1000 " | |
| | | | (4) Road running back from MALAKOFF FARM: Guns employed 1. (at L.10.b. 30.65) S.A.A expended 2,330 " | |
| | | | Enemy artillery fairly quiet during day (25th) but retaliated freely heavily to our m.g. shoot. | |
| | 25.7.17 | 6 a.m | The following gun positions were relieved by guns of No. 101 m.g.Coy on the night of 25/26/7/17 viz:- Nos. 3. 4. 6. 7. 19. 25. 24. and 36. | |
| | 26.7.17 | 6 a.m. | 2nd Lt. B.M.Perry was responsible for the relief of Nos. 3. 4. 6. 7 & 19. (B.1. Subsection). One man for each gun remained behind with relieving team for instructional purposes, and the nos. one proceeded under 2nd Lt. B.M.Perry to Transport lines HAMELET with the trader guns. The remainder of the personnel reported to Coy H.Q. as carrying party for the relief of the remaining guns on the following night. | |
| | | | 2nd Lt. O.B.Drew was responsible for the relief of Nos. 25. 24 & 36 positions in B.2. Subsector, and after relief proceed with the numbers one to Transport lines with guns etc. on limbers. One man for team remained with relieving team of 101 M.G Coy and the remainder of the men proceeded to Coy H.Q. | |

J.B. Anglesea Lt.
O.C 102 M.G. Coy.

# WAR DIARY

of 102 M.G. Coy.

## INTELLIGENCE SUMMARY.

Vol XVI

Army Form C. 2118.

| Place | Date | Hour | Summary of Events and Information | Remarks and references to Appendices |
|---|---|---|---|---|
| | 25/7/17 6am to 26/7/17 6am | | An advance party of HQ 101 MGC & 1 number team were attached to the following Battalions — nos. 14, 12, 17, 21st, 9, 6, 10a, 22, 23, for instructional purposes. They were met at dump and taken to the positions by baton party.<br><br>101 M.G. Coy took over the transport lines of 102 M.G. Coy on morning of 26th when Transport of 102 M.G.C. proceeded to and took over the lines vacated by 101 M.G. Coy near BERNES — R.34.d. I.O. — But 17th Division was responsible for the Transport move. | Ref. was Sheet 62C NE |
| | 26/7/17 6am to 27/7/17 6am | | The remainder of the guns of 102 M.G. Coy were relieved by guns of 101 M.G. Coy as follows:— (on night of 26/27/7/17.)<br>2nd Lieut. Swithin was responsible for relief of nos. 23, 22, & 21st. A carrying party of 3 n.c.o's & 18 men awaited these gun teams to carry out their kit when relieved to L.4.a.8.1. where they were met by limbers, and proceeded to BERNES.<br><br>2nd Lt. J.C.K. Chase was responsible for the relief nos 12 & 17 positions. The incoming teams at 9.30pm at L.10 a.1.2. and conducted limbers to 12 & 17 positions. These teams when relieved "limbered up" on 102 M.G. Coy limbers at no. 17 position and proceeded to transport lines at BERNES under 2nd Lt. J.C.K. Chase.<br><br>H.G. Anderson<br>/lt. 102 M.G. Coy | |

# WAR DIARY of 102 M.G. Coy.
## INTELLIGENCE SUMMARY

Army Form C. 2118.

Vol XVI

| Place | Date | Hour | Summary of Events and Information | Remarks and references to Appendices |
|---|---|---|---|---|
| | 26/7/17 | 6 am | Guides from no 102 9.9.14. met relieving teams at Right subsector H.Q. | Ref Trench Sheet 62C NE |
| | 27/7/17 | 9.30 am | were gun for no. 14 position was offloaded. He leader then proceeded to a dump near ULLERET. On relief no 102 & 9 guns tested guns shot up this limber which carries them to L.16.a.1.2. where they were met by limber of 102 M.G. Coy. when the 3 guns proceeded to BERNES. Tent Goltsterling was responsible for the relief. Coy Hqrs. Closed on relief being reports complete. | |
| BERNES | 28/7/17 | | Bombing of Beaurin Leagers. Shewing lists of detonations in personnel us | |
| | 28/7/17 | | Equipment so and small arms. Bayonet Fixing Battle. Map Reading for O.R.s. Inspection of Anti Gas appliances by N.C.O. from Divisional Anti Gas School. | |
| | 30/7/17 | | Stoppages, advances drill. Revolver practice on Range & Map Reading Lecture for Officers & N.C.O's. | |
| | 31/7/17 | | Gun drill. Revolver practice. | |

R.S. Robinson Lt
O.C. no 102 M.G. Coy.

Army Form C. 2118.

# WAR DIARY
of No 102 M.G. Coy
## INTELLIGENCE SUMMARY.
(Erase heading not required.)

Vol XVII

| Place | Date | Hour | Summary of Events and Information | Remarks and references to Appendices |
|---|---|---|---|---|
| BERNES | 1.9.17 Aug 1 | 9.30 am | Section parades under Section Officers in morning arranging Gun Kit, and preparing for "night scheme". | Ref. Maps Sheet 62° SE & 62° SW. |
| | | 12 noon | Night scheme postponed on warning orders received to go into line, earlier than anticipated. | |
| | Aug 2 | 9.30 am | Inspection of Coy by Company Commander. | |
| | | 10 am | Revolver practice on Range. | |
| | | 2 pm | Cleaning of Gun kit completed. One officer per section reconnoitres A Section and roads thereto in afternoon. Gun Rations drawn. An advance party of 1 man per Gun team moved into line and attached to teams of No 103 M.G. Coy in "A" Section. | |
| | 3/8/17 | 9.30 am | Inspection by Coy Commander. Coy relieves No Guns of No 103 m.G. Coy in A Section. 34th Divn front. Coy.H.Q at R5a 23. (62°SE) B & D Sections on night, A & D Sections as follows. | |
| | 4/9/17 | 6 am | Very quiet night. 10 pm - 11 pm 3rd intermittent shelling of ths TUNULOUS. | |
| | 4-8-17 to 5-8-17 | 6am 6am | Machine Gun fire carried out by us from 9pm to 1am on G34a & BELLE COPSE (3000 Rounds) G21a Coy H.Q. & track junction (3000 Rds) WATLING STREET (3350 Rds). Enemy replied to our shoot by "burst for burst" on Dragoon Post, which to a minute longer for hostile m.g. fire. From 6pm to 12 midnight 45 enemy shells burst the TUNULOUS, DRAGOON POST & BERTAUCOURT | |

H.B. Anderson
O/C 102 M.G. Coy.

# WAR DIARY

## of No 102 M. G. Coy.

### INTELLIGENCE SUMMARY.

Army Form C. 2118.

Vol XVII

| Place | Date | Hour | Summary of Events and Information | Remarks and references to Appendices |
|---|---|---|---|---|
| A Sector in 34 Divn. | 5-8-17 6am to 6-8-17 6am | | From 9.30pm 5th to 1am 6th we carried out m.g. fire on ST HELENE ROAD (7000 Rounds) and ELEVEN TREES (1250 Rounds). Enemy attitude quiet, never simulated firing of the Tumulous. One hostile m.g. replied to our m.g. shoot from direction of ST HELENE TRENCH. Casualties nil. | |
| -"- | 6-8-17 6am to 7-8-17 6am | | No firing was done by our guns. LE VERGUIER, JEANCOURT and the intervening ground were shelled between 9am & 2pm 6th and at 9pm - 11pm 6th enemy artillery active on RED WOOD, the Tumulous and valley East of PONTRU. Enemy planes engaged and driven back by anti aircraft fire at 9am & 10.30 am 6/8/17. Casualties nil. Great work done in improving gun positions. | |
| | 7-8-17 6am to 8-8-17 6am | | We carried out retaliating m.g. fire by 2 guns at DING POST and RB a 5.9 on hostile m.g's at LITTLE BILL and junction of trench of WATLING STREET at Stand to evening and morning. Each hostile burst was replied to by 5 bursts. The amount of enemy guns silence being only fired about 10% of their usual. Mobile artillery very quiet. | |

H.S. Anderson Lieut for
O/c. 102 M.G. Coy.

# WAR DIARY
## of No 102 M. G. Coy.
### INTELLIGENCE SUMMARY.

Army Form C. 2118.

*(Erase heading not required.)*

Instructions regarding War Diaries and Intelligence Summaries are contained in F. S. Regs., Part II. and the Staff Manual respectively. Title pages will be prepared in manuscript.

| Place | Date | Hour | Summary of Events and Information | Remarks and references to Appendices |
|---|---|---|---|---|
| A Section 3H.Q. un III Corps. | 9-8-17 6am to 9-8-17 6am. | | Retaliatory fire carried out on enemy M.G. at G.27.c.9.5. and evening thereto. 250 Rounds fired and job silenced. This gun was not fire again during the night. Artillery quiet except for intermittent light shelling of outposts. Work on our gun positions continued. | |
| | 9-8-17 to 10-8-17 | 6am. | M.G. fire was carried out on suspected hostile machine gun at G.27d.9.5. at Wandles evening and morning, 250 Rds expended. – Enemy gun only fired 250 rounds. We also fired on tracks in M.36.d.20. between 9pm – 10pm 9? Usual Shelling of TOMBOIS also ASCENSION FARM. We fired 250 Rounds from area position in PONTRU at hostile aircraft which was seen off. | |
| | | 8am. | Warning received that the 102 Bde was being relieved by 103 Bde on night of 10/10/11. An advance party of men under one Sub: from 103 M.G. Coy were attached to each of our Guns in afternoon. | |
| | | | 103 M.G. Coy relieved 102 Coy on night of 10th/11th. On relief the Coy proceeded to Transport Lines at BERNES | |
| | 11-8-17 12-8-17 | | Kit-Inspection, Checking Guns &c &c. Reading of Army Acts. Working party of 50 O.R. under 2/Lt J.Robinson proceeded to VENDELLES on Road Repairs. | |

J. S. Anderson Lieut.
for O/c 102 M.G. Coy.

# WAR DIARY
## or
## INTELLIGENCE SUMMARY
(Erase heading not required)

Army Form C. 2118.

of No 102 M.G Coy.

Vol XVII

| Place | Date | Hour | Summary of Events and Information | Remarks and references to Appendices |
|---|---|---|---|---|
| BERNES | 12/8/17 | | Warning order received that 102 M.G. Coy would relieve 16 Coy of No 101 M.G. Coy in B Section 34th Divn. front on night of 13/14th. Advance party of 7 men per gun team proceeds to B Section and attached 1 men to each team of 101 M.G. Coy for instructions. | Ref NAUROY Sheet 20000 |
| | 13.8.17 | | Baths for Coy in morning. Reading of Army Act. Coy relieved 16 Guns of No. 101 M.G. Coy in B Section 34th Divn. in the following position. No 3. No 4. No 6. No 7. No 12. No 17. No 9. No 10A. No 22. No 23. No 36. No 23. TOINE. ORCHARD No 21A. Nos. 3, 4, 6 & 7 Position, B Section, 9, 10 & 12 & 17 Position C Section. 36. 25. TOINE & ORCHARD Position A Section took over Nos. 21A. 22. 23 & 24 position. Transport moved to Haurings at HAMELET. | |
| B.Sector 34th Divn | 14.8.17 | 6am | No 10A position was shelled at 11.15am & 13th at 2.30 am and from 2.55-3.5 am Casualties nil. | |
| | 14.8.17 | 6am | We fired 500 Rounds at COLOGNE FARM 9/m to 10.15 pm 15t Enemy artillery very quiet, Little machine gun very active against our | |
| | 15/9/17 | 6am | aircraft | |

N. J. Anderson Lieut fr
9/102 M.G Coy

Army Form C. 2118.

# WAR DIARY of No. 102 M.G. Coy.

## INTELLIGENCE SUMMARY
*(Erase heading not required).*

Vol XII

Instructions regarding War Diaries and Intelligence Summaries are contained in F.S. Regs., Part II. and the Staff Manual respectively. Title pages will be prepared in manuscript.

| Place | Date | Hour | Summary of Events and Information | Remarks and references to Appendices |
|---|---|---|---|---|
| Bléin | 15.8.17 | 6 am | M.G. fire was carried out by us as follows. | Ref. NAUROY sheet 1/20000. |
| | | | On tracks in BUCKSHOT RAVINE and C.14.a.9.E. 9000 Rounds expended 1 am to 3.30 am | |
| | 16.8.17 | 6 am | On Gap Cut. by our Artillery in enemy wire at G.1.d.2.1. 4000 Rounds. 1 am to 5 am. | |
| | | | Enemy artillery shelled the CHATEAU L.23.C. at 9.15 am and retaliated to our Artillery shoot. 1 am to 1.20 am on HARGICOURT. Enemy aircraft busy but prevented from crossing our lines by accurate shooting of anti-aircraft batteries. Enemy machine guns quiet during the night. |  |
| | | | Our machine gun moved from ORCHARD POST to half way up Communication Trench of "LITTLE BENJAMIN" to Coon standing patrol at 1.0 am. returning to ORCHARD POST after warning "sentries". | |
| | | | A large fire was observed in ST QUENTIN 10 pm to midnight. | |
| | | | Our Artillery continued wire cutting. | |
| | 16.8.17 | 6 am | From 10 n/a nights 16 4.30 am intermittent m.g. fire was kept up on Gaps | |
| | 17.8.17 | 6 am | in hostile wire at G.7.6.5.0. G.13.d.9.5.80. L.6.C.85.15. G.1.d.2.1. Gun fires were employed and 14,500 Rounds S.A.A. expended. | |
| | 17.8.17 | 6 am | Our Artillery continued cutting and damaging enemy's trenches wire. | |
| | 18.8.17 | 6 am | During the night intermittent machine gun fire was kept up on the gaps in wire caused by our artillery. 5 guns were employed and 20,000 Rounds S.A.A. expended. | |

M.G. Anderson Lieut. For
O/C. 102 M.G. Coy.

Army Form C. 2118.

## WAR DIARY
or
## INTELLIGENCE SUMMARY.
(Erase heading not required)

of No 102 M.G.Coy.

| Place | Date | Hour | Summary of Events and Information | Remarks and references to Appendices |
|---|---|---|---|---|
| B Section Nurlu | 17/8/17 to 31st Aug - 18/8/17 | 6 am | Hostile Artillery fairly quiet except for usual shelling of the S.L.G. | Ref NAUROY Sheet 1/20000 |
| | 18/8/17 to 19/8/17 | 6 am to 6 am | No firing was done by us on account of our Infantry patrols routing & clearing damaged enemy wires &c. Hostile Artillery was active against the S.L.G., HARGICOURT & VILLERET VILLAGES and our outpost line. Enemy aircraft were active but accurate shooting by our anti aircraft batteries kept them from coming within machine gun range. | |
| | 19/8/17 to 20/8/17 | 6 am 6 am | No firing done by us. Enemy aircraft were again active but hostile artillery shown about the usual activity. One of our Aeroplanes was observed to be shot down when over enemy lines at 7.55 pm 19/8. | |
| | 20/8/17 to 21/8/17 | 6 am to 6 am | The damaged hostile wire was pretty thoroughly throughout the night by the new machine gun — 12000 Rounds fired. At 8.30 pm a Party of 25 Germans was observed at the N.W Corner of RUGY WOOD. Our Vickers gun at no 36 position opened fire on them fairly apparently with good effect, but owing to the weak visibility to observe accurately. | |

N.G. Anderson Lieut.
for O/C 102 m.G.Coy.

Army Form C. 2118.

# WAR DIARY
## of 102
# INTELLIGENCE SUMMARY.
(Erase heading not required.)

Instructions regarding War Diaries and Intelligence Summaries are contained in F. S. Regs., Part II. and the Staff Manual respectively. Title pages will be prepared in manuscript.

| Place | Date | Hour | Summary of Events and Information | Remarks and references to Appendices |
|---|---|---|---|---|
| Blécin 3½ Div | 21.8.17 | 6 a.m. to 6 a.m. | We carried out intermittent machine gun fire on enemy hostile wire from 1 a.m. to 6 a.m. 22nd. 3500 rounds fired. | Ref NAUROY sheet 2000 |
|  | 22.8.17 | 6 a.m. | At 1.15 a.m. 22nd 300 rounds were fired in response to S.O.S. signal. VILLERET and outposts received usual amount of shelling. At 1 a.m. 22nd in reply to a rocket bursting into 3 Red lights, enemy artillery commenced an intense bombardment of HARGICOURT with shells of all calibres lasting till 1.30 a.m. This village and again heavily shelled 3 a.m. to 3.15 a.m. Hostile aircraft went again busy during the day. One plane was shot down by anti aircraft guns at 11.30 a.m. to 3.15. |  |
|  | 22.8.17 | 6 a.m. | We again kept enemy hostile wire throughout the night. 3500 Rounds expended. Accurate bursts of MG enemy observed near RUBY WOOD. MG fires on by our MG's gun at no 36 position with apparently good effect. |  |
|  | 23.8.17 | 6 a.m. | HARGICOURT and SLAG 2 posts were very heavily shelled by the enemy from 4.20 p.m. to 7.30 p.m. 23rd by No. 23 gun position. One early damaged by a direct hit and bits deadline on suffy body wounded. |  |
|  | 24.8.17 | 6 a.m. | Throughout the night our machine guns kept up an intermittent fire on enemy damaged enemy wire — 3060 rounds being expended. Our "S.O.S." signals were observed at 1.30 a.m. & 3.30 a.m. and 3000 rounds were fired in response thereto at COLOGNE FARM, POND COPSE & UNNAMED FARM. No hostile infantry action took place. |  |

H.S. Anderson L.t Col
O/C 102 M.G.C.

# WAR DIARY
## or
## INTELLIGENCE SUMMARY.
(Erase heading not required.)

Army Form C. 2118.

| Place | Date | Hour | Summary of Events and Information | Remarks and references to Appendices |
|---|---|---|---|---|
| Bletar 3½ Divr. | 23/9/1. | | In accordance with Divisional orders previously issued, which has previously been made by them in an old Infantry post in Sunken Road at L.17.6.30.30. (Being relieved in afternoon position by 6 guns of No 103 M.G. Coy) his Battery of 8 guns took former command of the Divisional machine gun officers at 4 p.m. and were known as "D GROUP" and were under the command of Capt. I.R. PIPER M.C. (O.C. Coy) the object of this group was to assist in covering the Infantry attack on COLOGNE RIDGE by a Creeping M.G. Barrage and to put down S.O.S Barrage in front of the captured trenches when required. <br><br> C & D Sections (8 guns) remained in their defensive positions in left subsector for the defence of the line and came under the orders of G.O.C. 101st Infantry Brigade. (C & D section were then commanded by Lieut H.G. Anderson (H.Q. at COTE WOOD). <br><br> Reports were received from the Infantry that the enemy was repairing his wire in front of POND & ORCHARD TRENCHES, and accordingly 3 Vickers guns at no 36 position JOINE & ORCHARD posts fired 600 rounds on to this wire during the night of 23/24/9. The Infantry afterwards reported that practically was experienced in getting through the wire, and (as he had also decreed the enemy as to the time of the attack) prisoners stated that the eight had afforded "so ordinary" that the special "counter attacking" troops "stood down" one hour before our attack commenced. | Ref. GILLEMONT FARM Sheet 62 D.D. |

H.G. Anderson Lieut
for O/C. 102 M.G. Coy.

# WAR DIARY
## of No. 102 M.G. Coy.
## INTELLIGENCE SUMMARY.

Army Form C. 2118.

Vol XVII

| Place | Date | Hour | Summary of Events and Information | Remarks and references to Appendices |
|---|---|---|---|---|
| | 25/26th /8/17 | 8 p.m. | The barrage guns were laid on their first barrage lines at 8 pm 25th. Zero hour was at 4.30 am 26th when the guns of D Group opened fire. Rate & lines of firing are shown in attached orders marked appendix I, the barrage lines are col: red in attached Map (appendix VI) | Ref FILLEHONT FARM Sheet 10:0:0. |
| | 26/7/17 | 8 am | Report received that all objectives has been taken by the Infantry. 101st Infantry Brigade asked that 2 of our guns should be attached to the Infantry in forward positions to repele counter attacks by sneep fire. A later message ordered that the team and an officer should go forward with these guns. 2nd Lt. D.D Lead + 2 teams of C Section moved up into positions in RIFLEMAN & POND TRENCHES at midday 27/9/17. A warning was received that a minor operation would be carried out on night of 26/27th to capture a part of RIFLEMAN TRENCH which was still held by the enemy. "D Group" of barrage guns was ordered to put down a flank barrage to protect right flank. Zero hour was first given as 12.30 am then at 1.30 am and finally at 3.0 am 27/8. The barrage was carried out by machine gun and artillery but the infantry attack did not take place nothing having marked their jumping off positions in time. Three guns on left defensive position carried out intermittent fire throughout the night 26/7th on a line QUENNEMONT FARM, QUENNEY COPSE to prevent movement of enemy's left flank. | |

H.G. Anderson Lieut
for O/c 102 M.G. Coy.

Army Form C. 2118.

# WAR DIARY
or
## INTELLIGENCE SUMMARY. of 102 M.G. Coy.
Vol XVI
(Erase heading not required.)

Instructions regarding War Diaries and Intelligence Summaries are contained in F.S. Regs., Part II. and the Staff Manual respectively. Title pages will be prepared in manuscript.

| Place | Date | Hour | Summary of Events and Information | Remarks and references to Appendices |
|---|---|---|---|---|
| | 26/9/17 | 3.45 am | At 3.45 am "SOS" signals was observed and the Guns of D Group were switched on to "SOS" line in accordance with D.M.G.O's instructions and rapid fire was kept up for about 5 minutes and then a slower rate of fire was maintained for one hour. There was a general tendency on the part of the numbers one(1) to be influenced by the firing of the Battery and other machine guns and conforming to their rate of fire instead of carrying out their instructions. In all barrage 141000 rounds S.A.A. were fired by D Group. Faulty S.A.A. (of which "RL" mark was the worst) caused a good deal of trouble. All the means were gone by word of mouth which was satisfactory. The front was connected to the D.M.G.O's headquarters by Telephone. Faulty laying by the wires caused some little trouble but otherwise connection was not broken by hostile shelling. Intelligence was very slow in getting through from the Infantry and it was 8 am 26th before the situation was known. The setting of watches for the T was was an important factor. It was found necessary to rifle the guns every 3 or 4 belts and even then the guns got overheated. Wooden Toe Boards taken from Mule nets to prevent the Tripod legs from slipping. Tensioning scale proved invaluable. | Ref HILLERTON FAREY ghost 10000

H.S. Anderson Lt. O/C 102 M.G. Coy. |

# WAR DIARY
## INTELLIGENCE SUMMARY of 102 M.G. Coy.

Army Form C. 2118.

Vol XII

| Place | Date | Hour | Summary of Events and Information | Remarks and references to Appendices |
|---|---|---|---|---|
| | | | All Belt filling was done by hand. Watertight belts proved very stiff and it was a great strain on the men filling the belts to keep the Ammunition supply up. Captured German Belts were used as a reserve. No screens were used to conceal the flash of the guns, but the guns had a camouflage covering. No attempt was made by the enemy's artillery to systematically search for the front of Barrage Guns, although there were seventy machine guns on a half mile front and none were distant than 800-900 yards from the enemy. Only a few stray shells fell near the positions and no Casualties were caused. A detailed appendix is being drawn up giving details of appearances gained and technical difficulties overcome. | Ref GILLEMONT WOOD 10000. |
| | 28.9.17 | | The Coy has been in the line practically continuously since Aug 3rd including preliminary bombardment + day of attack. To Steinberg Line the remaining 2 guns of C Section moved forward soon relieved 2 of D, D.E.D. and his 2 gun teams in RIFLEMAN + POND TRENCHES. During the 48 hours tour of duty of 2nd D. News 2 guns, the Barrage was killed and his troops seriously wounded. The captured trenches were clearly observed and all movement actively sniped with 77mm Shells. The Trenches were very wet and muddy owing to the incessant rain, but no cases of "Trench feet" were reported. | |

M.G. Anderson
O/C 102 M.G. Coy.

Army Form C. 2118.

WAR DIARY of No. 102 M.G. Coy
or
INTELLIGENCE SUMMARY.
(Erase heading not required)

Vol XVII

| Place | Date | Hour | Summary of Events and Information | Remarks and references to Appendices |
|---|---|---|---|---|
| Bledin | 29/8/17. | | D Section was relieved in left sector and Kneuflis moved to D Troop and relieved B Section. B Section took over defensive positions in Centre Sector. | |
| | 30/31. | | A Section relieved C Section in defensive positions in Centre Sector. C Section took over positions in D Troop Trenches by A Section. | |

H.S. Anderson Lt.
for O/C 102 M.G. Coy.

APPENDIX "A" to War Diary Vol XVII Aug 1917
of No. 102 M.G. Coy.

## Fire Orders for D Group.

1. Zero hour will be 4.30 am 26th Aug 1917.

2. D Group will fire as follows:-
   Zero to Zero + 4 mins    "A" Barrage.
   Zero + 4 mins to Zero + 10 mins "B"   —"—
   Zero + 10 mins to Zero + 40 mins "C"  —"—

3. Barrage Charts for each gun have been issued.

4. Zero hour will be 4.30 am on Sunday 26th Aug. 1917.
   Times of firing will therefore be
   
   4.30 am - 4.34 am    "A" barrage
   4.34 am - 4.40 am    "B" barrage
   4.40 am - 5.10 am    "C" barrage
   5.10 am.  Guns will remain laid on "S.O.S." line

### RATE OF FIRE

Zero to Zero + 20 mins.
   All guns fire at maximum rate of fire
   i.e. 3 belts in 4 minutes, i.e. 15 belts.

Zero + 20 mins to Zero + 30 mins.
   1 Belt per gun per 3 mins, i.e. 3½ belts.

Zero + 30 to Zero + 40 mins.
   All guns will fire at the rate of one
   belt per 6 minutes

Zero + 40 mins cease fire and lay on S.O.S. lines

During such times as guns are laid on
S.O.S. lines, not more than one gun per
group will be taken out of action whether for
cleaning or any other purpose without reference
to O.C. Coy.

Guns firing for S.O.S. will fire at maximum
rate of fire.

Appendix A contd. p II

6. All Guns will traverse one degree right and one degree left of Zero line.

7. (a) A Sentry will be on duty to look out for S.O.S. signals all the time.

(b) A number one will be on duty at each gun

(c) An officer will be on duty at each group all the time.

(d) All guns will be half loaded.

(e) "SOS" Signal will be a rifle grenade bursting into two red and 2 white stars

8. All guns to be laid by 8 p.m. on 25th inst

Signed. J. R. PYPER. Capt
O/c D Group
102 M.G.C.

APPENDIX B
To WAR DIARY Vol XVII Aug 1918
of 102 M.G. Coy

Part of GILLEMONT FARM Sheet
Ed I Scale 1:10,000

Appendix C. to War Diary Vol XVII Aug 1917
of No. 102 M.G. Coy

26.8.17.

Barrage Order
D Group.

D. Group will assist a minor attack by putting up a barrage to protect right flank.

Zero 1.30 am 27th inst

Charts showing each phase of fire have been issued to guns

Each gun will be switched from its present S.O.S. line to new barrage line and a steel picket driven into table as a traversing stop. Gun will then be at once switched to old S.O.S. line where a traversing stop will also be driven in (a steel one). By swinging gun either to right or left stop, Right or Left S.o.S. line or the new barrage line can be laid on at once.

If "S.o.S." goes up during Barrage at 1.30 am all guns at once switch to left traversing stop and fire at medium rate of fire.

When "one belt per minute" rate of fire is ordered, it does not mean that 250 rounds will be blazed off in the first 15 seconds and no fire be produced for the last 45 seconds of the minute.

Short & frequent bursts of say 15 rounds are much more efficient. This order will be strictly carried out

The action of "D" Group depends on orders issued by O.C. Group or the officer acting for him.

If the "S.o.S." is given and no one else is firing, D Group will fire. The action of the Cavalry Barrage guns does not concern D Group

Signed "J.R. PYPER. Capt.

# WAR DIARY or INTELLIGENCE SUMMARY

Army Form C. 2118.

102 M.G. Coy.

| Place | Date | Hour | Summary of Events and Information | Remarks and references to Appendices |
|---|---|---|---|---|
| | 1/3/17 | | Subsection on Pont Ferme relieved by night by 101st Coy and went back to barrage position at L.11.d.33 | Ref NAUROY sheet Colition 2. 1/20000 |
| | 4/5 | night | B section relieved in VILLARET position by 101st Coy and went to HERVILLY to prepare to take part in operation for the capture of RAILWAY and FARM TRENCHES. | |
| | 6/8/7 | | Orders received for D group (A + C section) to move to party dug emplacements near MOLLY POST in front of GRAND RIEL FARM. | |
| | 7/5 | night 10pm | B section guns allotted to 2nd & 4th Battalions Tyneside Scottish came into position and were now under the orders of the C.O. of these Battalions. | |

[signature] Lieut
for O.C. 102 M.G. Coy.

# WAR DIARY
## or
## INTELLIGENCE SUMMARY.

Army Form C. 2118.

| Place | Date | Hour | Summary of Events and Information | Remarks and references to Appendices |
|---|---|---|---|---|
| | 8/9/1917 | | The 102 n̂d Brigade attacked at 12.15 a.m. main objectives captured but support of FARM TRENCH remained untaken as gun covering excavation into the VILLARET rally. | |
| | | | NOTE Two of B section guns & teams with the 2nd Battalion became out of action. | |
| | | | One gun met 14 H Battalion establishes itself in RAILWAY TRENCH and did good work. | |
| | | | One gun for protection of right flank of objective west side a position in MARTIN POST. This is the leftmost trying to ensure the after one gun & light was seriously damaged and its men killed. The position was changed for one in MER POST where the gun stayed till relieved by a gun of 101st Bn on night of 11/12 | |

**WAR DIARY**
*or*
**INTELLIGENCE SUMMARY.** of 102 M.G.C.

Army Form C. 2118.

| Place | Date | Hour | Summary of Events and Information | Remarks and references to Appendices |
|---|---|---|---|---|
| | night 30/11 | | NOTE (continued). D. Coy. co-operated in Zero operation by firing for 20 minutes (at Zero - Zero +20) then every half hour up till 7.35 a.m. 81,000 rounds were fired. | Ref. I.N.H./B.X. Official Sheet Belgium 2. 1/20,000 |
| | night 30/11 | | Attack by 3rd Battn. Tyneside Scottish in FARM TRENCH. All objectives taken & held. D. Coy. fired from Zero to Zero +10 intervals fire for about 20,000 rounds (S.A.A.) | |
| | night 1/12 | | Gun in RAILWAY TRENCH relieved by one of 101st Coy. that Coy. also relieved PIER POST gun and the distribution then was :- Egg Farm 1 2 section MOLLY POST gun damaged at 4.11 A | |

for O/C 102 M.G. Coy

**Army Form C. 2118.**

# WAR DIARY
## or
## INTELLIGENCE SUMMARY.

(Erase heading not required.)

Vol XII 2/102 May 17

Instructions regarding War Diaries and Intelligence Summaries are contained in F.S. Regs., Part II. and the Staff Manual respectively. Title pages will be prepared in manuscript.

| Place | Date | Hour | Summary of Events and Information | Remarks and references to Appendices |
|---|---|---|---|---|
| night 1/2.5.17 | | 11.12 p.m. | 1 subsection at KAFFIR COPSE and B.H. fountain. The other subsection also used for the same keep.<br><br>NOTE<br>Between a quarter of a million and three hundred thousand rounds S.A.A. was fired by the guns of the Company during the period under review.<br><br>It will be seen from the record that only four guns have been in action for 31 days.<br><br>Except after the first when 2 guns became out of action (a third was temporarily out of action but was repaired by F.O.D. | 24/5/17<br>Check this<br>Extra 2<br>+ 2 m |

J.B. Kenninough
for O/C 102 MGC

# WAR DIARY
## or
## INTELLIGENCE SUMMARY.

Army Form C. 2118.

*(Erase heading not required.)*

No. 102 M.G. Coy.

| Place | Date | Hour | Summary of Events and Information | Remarks and references to Appendices |
|---|---|---|---|---|
| | 13/10/17 | | All guns standing by in S.O.S. line. No firing done. Hostile artillery quite on the whole. | By GNAPOT General Staff N. Sector 2.B. 100 |
| | 16/7 | | Company motored from line in night of 16/17 & went back to HERVILLY. | |
| | 18/10 | | Change of all guns and emery and kit. | |
| | 20/7 | | Company returned 103 M.G. Coy in left sector. Position of guns as follows: | |
| | | | A section — | |
| | | | 1 gun LITTLE BENJAMIN | |
| | | | 1 gun BENJAMIN POST | |
| | | | 1 gun ORCHARD " | |
| | | | 1 gun TRONE | |
| | | | 1 gun QUARRY F29 c | |
| | | | B section — | |
| | | | C section — 1 gun HUZZAR POST | |
| | | | 1/2 gun RIFLERT TRENCH | |
| | | | 1 gun BOWER LANE | |
| | | | 1 gun QUARRY F29 d | |
| | | | D section — 2 gun ENFILADE TRENCH | |
| | | | 2 gun RUBYZANE | |
| | 21/7 | | One gun went forward to BENJAMIN POST. Sec I made aware of front of enemy aircraft by gun at ORCHARD road. BENJAMIN POST. Enemy artillery quiet. | |
| | 22/23 | | 3 gun of B sector, 1 gun of C sector, moved to Quarry L100 moved to BENJAMIN POST | |

[signatures]

for O/c 102 M.G. Coy.

# WAR DIARY
## INTELLIGENCE SUMMARY of N.Z. M.G.C.

Army Form C. 2118.

| Place | Date | Hour | Summary of Events and Information | Remarks and references to Appendices |
|---|---|---|---|---|
| | 22nd/29/1/17 | | Enemy artillery fire & barrage heavy. Sent to 6.15 am S.O.S rocket was observed at 5 am when our machine guns opened a fire. Was maintained on S.O.S line till 5.30 am. Firing ceased at 5.20 am. But no trace of any men fell at any of our position | Ref. MURRY Official Hist. issue 2nd 20 m? |
| | 23rd /30 | | No firing done by our machine guns. Our forward positions lightly shelled intermittently | |
| | 24th/1 | | 12.30 reports were firing on tracks & communication trench enemy lines from 10.15 pm to 11.45 pm | |
| | 25/2/6 | | No firing done. Enemy artillery quiet during the day but at 10 pm Lewis guns were heavily shelled without results for about ½ hour | |
| | 26/7/8 | | Company was relieved on the line by B. 13 M.G.C. On relief moved to BERNES and billets for the night | |
| | 27 | | Company entrained at BERNES for PERONNE. Billeted on JOCK ROAD. Transport and marched to DOINGT | |
| | 28 | | Standing by awaiting orders | |

W. Alexander
Capt OC 102 M.G. Coy

# WAR DIARY
## or
## INTELLIGENCE SUMMARY.

of M.G. Coy

Army Form C. 2118.

| Place | Date | Hour | Summary of Events and Information | Remarks and references to Appendices |
|---|---|---|---|---|
| | 29/9/17 | | Transport rode marched under 102nd Brigade Transport Officer to BAPAUME | |
| | 30/9/17 | | Entrained at FLAMICOURT - PERONNE at 2.20pm Detrained BOISLEUX-AU-MONT and marched to billets at BELLACOURT | |
| | 1/10/17 | | Transport route marched to BELLACOURT | |

J. Hindenberg Lt
for O/C 102 m.g. Coy.

# WAR DIARY
## INTELLIGENCE SUMMARY.

*(Erase heading not required.)*

Army Form C. 2118.

Vol XIX  of 102 M.G. Coy.

| Place | Date | Hour | Summary of Events and Information | Remarks and references to Appendices |
|---|---|---|---|---|
| BELLA-COURT | 1/10/17 | | Day spent cleaning up all Gun, Gun Lib. and men's personal kit. | |
| " | 2/10/17 | | Inspection of Coy. by Coy Commander. Programme of training commenced. ie. Physical training (Swedish), Squad drill. Lecture to N.C.Os. | |
| " | 3/10/17 | | Capt. J.R. Ryan. M.C. proceeded on leave to UK and Lieut J.R. Shuttleworth assumed command of the Coy. Second in Command assumed command of Division Commander. General training as laid down by Division Commander, ie Physical training, Swedish, Musketry, Flammenwerfer, Map Reading, Bayonet drill, N.C.Os — Lecture N.C.Os on overseeing duties NCO by O.C.M.G. Lectures to Officers, Lecture on Barrage methods by Lt. J.R. Shuttleworth. Officers lecture on Barrage methods by Lt. J.R. Shuttleworth. 10 Infantry drill and Physical training. | |
| " | 4/10/17 | | Coy Inspection by O.C Coy. Training carried on. Arm and Physical training and commencement of Gas Course. NCOs Map Reading Class under Lt. W.J. Anderton. Bombers NCOs Lecture on Ammunition by B.O.M. Officers lecture "Methods of Obtaining & Maintaining Elevation" by Lieut Shuttleworth. | |

J.R. Ryan
Capt
OC. 102 M.G. Coy.

# WAR DIARY
## INTELLIGENCE SUMMARY of No. 102 M.G. Coy

Army Form C. 2118.

Vol NT

| Place | Date | Hour | Summary of Events and Information | Remarks and references to Appendices |
|---|---|---|---|---|
| BELLA-COURT | 27/9/17 | | Sent A.G. Anderson forward to join British Mission with American Expeditionary Force CHAUMONT in accordance with orders received from A.G.<br><br>Sent P.H. Dixon forward on course of Transport Duties at Advanced Horse Transport Depot, ABBEVILLE.<br><br>Coy inspection by O.C. Coy and having continued training i.e. arms drill, & physical training & machine gun & Lewis gun targets.<br><br>Lewis N.C.O.s had carried class.<br><br>Lewis N.C.O.s lecture by Coy officers "Tactical use of M.G.s" — General arrangements of Authorities.<br><br>In accordance with Divisional Instructions extra personnel to follow joined the Coy from the Infantry Battalions of 102 Bde i.e. 9 men & 1 transport driver from each of 20th, 21st, 22nd, 23rd Bns. to be permanently attached. | |

J R Ryan Major
O.C. 102 Machine Gun Coy.

# WAR DIARY
## INTELLIGENCE SUMMARY of No 102 M.G. Coy

Army Form C. 2118.

Vol IX

| Place | Date | Hour | Summary of Events and Information | Remarks and references to Appendices |
|---|---|---|---|---|
| BELLA-COURT | 6/9/17 | | Training continued. Lecture by O.C. Coy. Demonstration of lecture to N.C.Os and Gun nos 1 & 2 in "Killing of Guns in Trench System". This was carried out on a Trench System near BASSEUX under Lieut J Rutherford. Lieut J Rutherford attended a lecture on the methods of warfare in YPRES AREA in Arkenton. Preparing for moving Barbed trailers &c. | |
| | 7/9/17 | | Coy and transport route marched to SAULTY STATION and entrained there for O.H. in accordance with 3rd Division Administrative Order no 19. | |
| | 8/9/17 | 3.45am | Arrived at PESELHOEK STATION, BELGIUM and detrained. Route marched to PEGWELL CAMP nr PROVEN turning G.O's orders received from 102nd Brigade that Coy would probably move forward a distance of 8 miles on the 9th. Inspection of feet and gas appliances and from Padsons Inspector of feet. | |

J.R. Pym Keppe

O/C 102 M.G. Coy.

# WAR DIARY
## INTELLIGENCE SUMMARY

Army Form C. 2118.

of No 102 M.G. Coy.  Vol XX

| Place | Date | Hour | Summary of Events and Information | Remarks and references to Appendices |
|---|---|---|---|---|
| PEGWELL CAMP PROVEN | 9/10/17 to 12/10/17 | | Training Squad drill and M.G. Barrage drill | Ref Sheet 28 NW |
| | 13/10/17 | | 102 Bde moved forward to MALAKOFF AREA and relieved No 10 Inf Bde in Divisional Reserve. 102 M.G. Coy entrained at PROVEN in afternoon, detrained at ELVERDINGHE and marched to SOLFERINO CAMP 13.22.E.7.5.. Transport proceeded from PROVEN to BRIDGE CAMP near ELVERDINGHE by route march | |
| | 14/10/17 | | Preparing guns and equipment for the line. Squadron of enemy aircraft bombed the neighbourhood of MALAKOFF AREA causing casualties to neighbouring Battalions & Transport. Officers reconnoitred the line. | |
| | 15/10/17 | | Coy marched from SOLFERINO CAMP B.45. N.W. to STRAY FARM and Bivouacked for the night. | |

T R Ryan Capt.
O/C 102 M.G. Coy.

# WAR DIARY
## or
## INTELLIGENCE SUMMARY.
*(Erase heading not required.)*

of No 102 M.G. Coy    Vol XIX    Army Form C. 2118.

| Place | Date | Hour | Summary of Events and Information | Remarks and references to Appendices |
|---|---|---|---|---|
| | 16/10/17 | | No 102 m.G. Coy relieved no 51 M.G. Coy with 2 sections on left sector and 103 M.G. Coy 2 section on the right sector on the night of 16/17th. Coy HQ at AU BON GITE. C Section on Right in front of FERDAN FARM D Section on Right in neighbourhood of WATERY STRING HOUSE A Section on Left at GRAVEL FARM and a TRANQUIL HOUSE B Section on Left at TRUEMYRE CROSSING. | Ref sheet 28 NW |
| | 17/17 | | An an Brigade Counter to back made with showers of rain over cert. 16 June near BARO'S CAUSEWAY near YSER CANAL for the purpose of carrying forward water. Rations sc. Enemy counter attack ensued. No. 101 & 240 M.G. Coys covered Barrage forward from Reserve. | |
| | 18/10/17 | | Coy HQ. moved to DOUBLE COURTS and DROPHOUSES. H.Q. staff and M.G Runners heavily gas shelled about 5 p.m. — Several casualties. Heavy rain during night. Enemy machine gun activity below normal. | |

J.R.Gow Lieut
O.C. 102 M.G. Coy

# WAR DIARY
## INTELLIGENCE SUMMARY

Army Form C. 2118.

of No. 102 M.G. Coy

| Place | Date | Hour | Summary of Events and Information | Remarks and references to Appendices |
|---|---|---|---|---|
| | 19/9/17 | | Coy HQ at PROHOUSES subjected to intermittent shelling. "C" Section had gun team out of action and several casualties. Men began to complain of trench feet. | Ref Sheet 28 N.W. |
| | 20/9/17 | | Artillery activity intense at dawn. B Section on left had gun damaged by shell fire and two men wounded on left. Anti aircraft became active. Weather conditions become worse | |
| | 21/9/17 | | At dawn B Section on left was relieved by 101 M.G.Coy and returned to STRAY FARM proceeding at dusk to anti aircraft positions protecting artillery batteries in BROEMBECK VALLEY. "A" Section was relieved by Section of 101 M.G. Coy and returned to STRAY FARM. Our troops were suffering from exposure, several men having to be sent to Divisional Rest. | |
| | 22/9/17 | | Attack by 3t Division at 5.30 am. 4 Guns attached to 24/27 N.F. subject by C Section. 4 Guns for close defence of own attack position supplied by D Section. Remaining guns (two) in Reserve. At Zero hour it commenced to rain. Under heavy bombardment the attack was made. Only information available shows all objectives had been captured. | |

T.R.Pepper Capt
O/C 102 M.G. Coy.

# WAR DIARY
## or
## INTELLIGENCE SUMMARY of 102 M.G. Coy

Army Form C. 2118.

| Place | Date | Hour | Summary of Events and Information | Remarks and references to Appendices |
|---|---|---|---|---|
| | 23/10/17 | | 102 Inf Bde was withdrawn and 102 M.G. Coy then came under the orders of G.O.C. 103 Inf. Bde. The same dispositions were held. Teams are becoming much reduced by casualties, and all available men had from company teams to relieve the 4 gun teams now in the line. | Ref sheet 28 NW |
| | 24/10/17 | | No. 102 M.G. Coy was relieved by no. 170 M.G. Coy and returned to STRAY FARM on night of 24/25/5. The men had been subjected to a very severe 24 hours from shelling and exposure due to NW gale and heavy rain. | |
| | 25/10/17 | | Marched to BOESINGHE STATION in morning and entrained at 2 p.m. Detrained at PROVEN and marched to billets at PEGWELL CAMP near PROVEN. Referred 102 Inf Bde. | |
| | 26/10/17 | | Resting and cleaning up at PEGWELL CAMP | |

J.R.Ryan Capt
O/C 102 M.G. Coy

Army Form C. 2118.

# WAR DIARY
## of
## INTELLIGENCE SUMMARY.

(Erase heading not required.) of No 102 M.G. Coy

Instructions regarding War Diaries and Intelligence Summaries are contained in F.S. Regs, Part II. and the Staff Manual respectively. Title pages will be prepared in manuscript.

| Place | Date | Hour | Summary of Events and Information | Remarks and references to Appendices |
|---|---|---|---|---|
| | 27/10/17 | | Advance party went forward billeting at BOISLEUX au MONT (XI Corps area). | |
| | 28/10/17 | | Church Parade in morning. Marched off at 3 p.m. to HOUDOURE Station and entrained. Were 6.30 p.m. | |
| | 29/10/17 | | Detrained early morning at BOISLEUX AU MONT Station and marched to ARGYLE CAMP No. BOISLEUX ↑ MONT | Ref Sheet LENS 11 to oo. |
| | 30/10/17 | | Preparing guns to go for the line. | |
| | 31/10/17 | | Officers reconnoitred the line, and an advance party of 8 O.R. reported to No 15st M.G. Coy in the line. | |

J.R.Ryan Capt.
O/c 102 M.G. Coy

APPENDIX II.
*********

## DISTRIBUTION STATEMENT.

| | | |
|---|---|---|
| Divisional Headquarters, | PROVEN. | F.1.c.2.0. (Northern Divisional Headquarters) |
| Headquarters, R.E. | | -do- |
| D.A.D.O.S. | | -do- |
| Headquarters, Divl. Train, | PROVEN, | E.12.d.3.7. |
| Mob. Vet. Section, | | -do- |

### P.2 AREA.

| | | |
|---|---|---|
| 101st Bde. Headquarters, | PENGE Camp, | X.27.a.4.6. |
| 1 Battalion, | PICCADILLY Camp, | X.20.d. |
| 1 " | PUTNEY Camp, | X.27.a. |
| 1 " | PENTON Camp, | F.8.a. |
| Machine Gun Coy. | PADDINGTON Camp, | F.3.a. |
| Trench Mortar Bty. | PLAISTOW Camp, | F.9.a. |
| 207th Fd.Co. R.E. | PRAED Camp, | F.9.a. |
| 104th Field Ambulance, | PORTLAND Camp, | X.28.a. |
| No. 2 Co. Div. Train, | PIGEON Camp, | F.14.a. |
| | POPLAR Camp, | F.2.a. |

### P.3. AREA.

| | | |
|---|---|---|
| 102nd Bde. Headquarters, | PORTSMOUTH Camp, | W.30.b. |
| 1 Battalion, | PURBROOK Camp, | W.29.c. |
| 1 " | PORCHESTER Camp, | E.5.b. |
| 1 " | PRIVET Camp, | X.25.c. |
| | PETWORTH Camp, | X.25.d. |
| Machine Gun Coy. | POINT Camp, | W.30.c. |
| Trench Mortar Bty. | PITT Camp, | W.30.d. |
| 208th Fd. Co. R.E. | PORTSDOWN Camp, | X.25.a. |
| 102nd Field Ambulance, | PORTSEA Camp, | F.1.b. |
| No.3 Co. Div. Train, | PORTOBELLO Camp, | W.30.d. |

### P.4. AREA.

| | | |
|---|---|---|
| 103rd Bde. Headquarters, | PENSHURST Camp, | E.11.c. |
| 1 Battalion, | PADDOCKWOOD Camp, | E.4.d. |
| 1 " | PLURENDEN Camp, | E.10.b. |
| 1 " | POLEHILL Camp, | E.10.a. |
| | PLUMSTEAD Camp, | E.10.a. |
| Machine Gun Coy. | PEGWELL Camp, | E.5.d. |
| Trench Mortar Bty. | PATCHAM Camp, | E.5.c. |
| 103rd Field Ambulance, | PURLEY Camp, | E.5.a. |
| 208th Fd. Co. R.E. | PILGRIM Camp, | E.4.c. |
| No.4 Coy. Div. Train, | PELERIN Camp, | E.4.c. |

--------------

| | | |
|---|---|---|
| 240th Machine Gun Coy. | POMPEY Camp, | E.12.d. |

SECRET.   TRAIN TIME TABLE - Move from VIth Corps Area to XIVth Corps Area.

| No. of Train. | Date. | Place of Entrainment. | Time of Departure. | Composition. | Place of Detrainment. | Remarks. |
|---|---|---|---|---|---|---|
| 1 | 7/10/17 | SAULTY. | 3.42 | 16th Royal Scots, less 1 Company, 1 Cooker and team. | PESELHOEK. | |
| 2 | " | BEAULETZ. | 4.06 | 101 Bde.H.Q., 1 Company, 1 Cooker and team of 15th Royal Scots, Bde.Signal Sec., 101 M.G.Coy. 101 T.M.Battery. | PROVEN. | |
| 3. | " | GOUY. | 5.08 | 10th Lincolns, less 1 Company, 1 Cooker and team. | HOPOUTRE. | |
| 4. | " | SAULTY. | 7.42 | 11th Suffolks, less 1 Company, 1 Cooker and team. | PESELHOEK. | |
| 5. | " | BEAULETZ. | 8.08. | 15th Royal Scots, less 1 Company, 1 Cooker and team. | PROVEN. | |
| 6. | " | GOUY. | 9.03 | 1 Company, 1 Cooker and team of 10th Lincs., No.2 Coy. Div.Train, 104th Field Ambulance. | HOPOUTRE. | |
| 7. | " | SAULTY. | 11.42 | 1 Coy., 1 Cooker and team of 15th Royal Scots, 1 Coy. 1 Cooker and team of 11th Suffs. 208th Fd. Co. R.E. | PESELHOEK. | |
| 8. | " | BEAULETZ. | 12.08 | 1 Coy., 1 Cooker and team of 24th N.F., No.4 Coy. Div.Train, 209th Fd.Co. R.E. | PROVEN. | |
| 9. | " | GOUY. | 12.53 | 1 Coy., 1 Cooker and team 21st N.F., 1nCoy., 1 Cooker and team 23rd N.F. 207th Fd.Co. R.E. | HOPOUTRE. | |

2.

| No. of Train. | Date. | Place of Entrainment. | Time of Departure. | Composition. | Place of Detrainment. | Remarks. |
|---|---|---|---|---|---|---|
| 10. | 7/10/17 | SAULTY. | 15.42 | 102 Bde.H.Q., 1 Coy, 1 Cooker and team of 20th N.F. Bde.Signal Sec. 102 M.G.Coy. 102 T.M.Battery. | PESELHOEK. | Parade ready to move at 6 P.M. O.B.C. 2014th Lt. ramdyn, ken at 4.45 P.M. Coy. Comdt. Kettle ...... Notice for trainmen to follow drop the arrival in ..... men in W's Dalmar report packs kits full, into Battle. |
| 11. | " | BEAULETZ. | 16.06 | 103 Bde.H.Q., 1 Coy., 1 Cooker and team of 9th N.F. Bde.Signal Sec. 103 M.G.Coy. 103 T.M.Battery. | PROVEN. | |
| 12. | " | GOUY. | 17.08 | 21st N.F. less 1 Company, 1 Cooker and team. | HOPOUTRE. | |
| 13. | " | SAULTY. | 19.42 | 20th N.F. less 1 Coy., 1 Cooker and team. | PESELHOEK. | |
| 14. | " | BEAULETZ. | 20.06 | 9th N.F. less 1 Coy., 1 Cooker and team. | PROVEN. | |
| 15. | " | GOUY. | 21.08 | 23rd N.F. less 1 Coy., 1 Cooker and team. | HOPOUTRE. | |
| 16. | " | SAULTY. | 23.42 | 22nd N.F. less 1 Coy., 1 Cooker and team. | PESELHOEK. | |
| 17. | 8/10/17 | BEAULETZ. | 0.06 | Div.H.Q. H.Q.R.E. H.Q. and 1 Section Div.Signals. | PROVEN. | |
| 18. | " | GOUY. | 1.08 | 25th N.F. less 1 Coy., 1 Cooker and team. | HOPOUTRE. | |
| 19. | " | SAULTY. | 3.42 | 1 Coy. 1 Cooker and team 22nd N.F. No.3 Co.Div.Train, 102nd Fd.Amb. | PESELHOEK. | |
| 20. | " | BEAULETZ. | 4.06 | 240th M.G.Coy. Div.Employment Co. H.Q.Div.Train. M.V.S. | PROVEN. | |

3.

| No. of Train. | Date. | Place of Entrainment. | Time of Departure. | Composition. | Place of Detrainment. | Remarks. |
|---|---|---|---|---|---|---|
| 21. | 8/10/17 | GOUY. | 5.08 | 26th N.F. less 1 Company, 1 Cooker and team. | HOPOUTRE. | |
| 22. | " | BEAUMETZ. | 8.06 | 24th N.F. less 1 Company, 1 Cooker and team. | PROVEN. | |
| 23. | " | GOUY. | 9.08 | 1 Company, 1 Cooker and team 25th N.F., 1 Company, 1 Cooker and team 26th N.F., 103rd Fd. Ambce. | HOPOUTRE. | |

# WAR DIARY
## INTELLIGENCE SUMMARY
(Erase heading not required.) of No. 102 M.G. Coy. Vol. 19

Army Form C. 2118.

| Place | Date | Hour | Summary of Events and Information | Remarks and references to Appendices |
|---|---|---|---|---|
| | 1/11/17 | | No 102 M.G. Coy relieved No 154 M.G. Coy (51st Division) with 8 Guns in left Brigade Sector, 34 Divn front. Two Guns from each Section carried out this Relief, and the remaining two teams per Section moved to transport lines and were in reserve. Coy H.Q. moved forward to N.16.b.2.8. The location of the teams taken over by guns teams are as follows. No.60 (i) 019.b 75.60; 60 (ii) 019.b 30.60; 60.A 019.c 75.80; 57 – 019.d 05.08. 58 020.c 50.50; 58 (ii) 020.c 70.48; 58 (iii) 020.c 25.30. 56 – 019.d 62.10. 59 019.b 60.95 | Ref Sheet 51/13 S.E. 1/20000 |
| | 2/11/17 | 6 am | Relief was completed without special incident. The night passed very quietly, only occasional intermittent machine Gun fire. No firing was done. | |
| | 2/11/17 | 6 am | Enemy was rather active with light trench mortars on the Right. 11:30am – 12 noon, evening extremely quiet, but machine guns were active during the night. | |
| | 3/11/17 | 6 am | Owing to night firing programme received two more guns were brought into the line, to be used chiefly in night firing work. The men for this work were drawn from the teams already in the line, in rotation, in order that 8 teams should be kept in reserve at transport lines, so that reliefs could be regularly carried out. | |
| | 3/11/17 | 6 am | Harras. fire was carried out on 0.15.c 20.60 from 10.30 pm – 12.30 am on 0.21.c 75.78. from 12.15 am to 2.15 am. | |
| | 4/11/17 | 6 am | Hostile Artillery was more active than usual between 8 am & 11 pm on our front line, a number of gas shells were also dropped. | |

For 102 M.G. Coy.

Army Form C. 2118.

# WAR DIARY
## or
## INTELLIGENCE SUMMARY.

of No 102 M.G. Coy

Vol XL

(Erase heading not required.)

Instructions regarding War Diaries and Intelligence Summaries are contained in F. S. Regs., Part II. and the Staff Manual respectively. Title pages will be prepared in manuscript.

| Place | Date | Hour | Summary of Events and Information | Remarks and references to Appendices |
|---|---|---|---|---|
| | 4.11.17 to 5.11.17 | 7am | Nos. 1 & 2 of Reserve Teams went into line and were attached to Gun teams for instruction. Nos. 1 & 2 also already in the line went back to Transport Lines. | Ref Sheet 51B SW |
| | 5.11.17 | 6am | 3000 Rounds were fired by 4 Guns on Factory 0.15c 90.45, Road junction 0.15c 20.75 and 0.26c 75.05 intermittently during the night. Hostile activity normal. Snipers were active apparently from direction of ST ROBARTS QUARRY | |
| | 5.11.17 to 6.11.17 | 7pm 6am | Indirect night fire was carried out by 2 Guns on Dumps at 0.27 B 18.85" and Two Roads 0.27c 30.90. 3000 Rounds fired in neighbourhood of 0.20G 45.30. Enemy was active with Trench Mortars against our trenches intermittently throughout the night. Enemy machine guns were active against our trenches intermittently throughout the night. | |
| | 6.11.17 to 7.11.17 | 7am 6am | Indirect m.g. fire was carried out by 3 Guns intermittently throughout the night on 0.26c 75.05 and 0.27c 30.90, 700.0 Rounds being fired. Hostile artillery was occasionally active on APE & 13.15 TRENCHES between 9am & 10am ground between GANNET & EGRET TRENCHES was shelled from direction of ST ROBARTS QUARRY. The night passed quietly except for usual enemy machine gun fire. | |
| | 7.11.17 to 8.11.17 | 6am 6am | 700.0 Rds fired on two Roads 0.21.6 75.18 & Road Junction 0.26c 75.04 intermittently throughout night. Artillery activity of Enemy slightly increased | |

[signature]
O.C. 102 M.G. Coy

Army Form C. 2118.

# WAR DIARY
## or
## INTELLIGENCE SUMMARY of No 102 M.G. Coy
(Erase heading not required.)

Instructions regarding War Diaries and Intelligence Summaries are contained in F.S. Regs., Part II. and the Staff Manual respectively. Title pages will be prepared in manuscript.

Vol XX

| Place | Date | Hour | Summary of Events and Information | Remarks and references to Appendices |
|---|---|---|---|---|
| Poperinghe | 8/11/17 | | No I & J Sections in Reserve relieved No. 1 & H Sections in the line in afternoon | Ref. Sheet 27/5 S.W. |
| | 9/11/17 | 6am | 1000 Rounds fired during the night on enemy's instructions in accordance with Bn G.O's instructions. Enemy artillery activity normal. | |
| | 9/11/17 | 6pm | Sections in the line were relieved by Sections in reserve on afternoon of 9/11/17. | |
| | 9/11/17 | 6am | 4000 Rounds fired during the night on 026c40.10, and 032a45.70 | |
| | 10/11/17 | 6pm | Enemy artillery and machine gun activity normal. | |
| | 10/11/17 | 6am | Night firing continued. 8000 Rounds being fired on H.Q. dugouts at 026d 80.65 and four Roads 0.27c 30.90 | |
| | 11/11/17 | 6am | Enemy artillery & quiet. | |
| | 11/11/17 | 6am | Night firing carried out by 4 guns on O.P.s 032B 45.00 & 0.32a 20.00 intermittently throughout the night - 7000 Rounds expended. | |
| | 12/11/17 | 6am | Enemy artillery quiet but trench mortars very active between 5.30pm - 6.30pm also from 8pm to 9pm to 11h Enemy machine guns exceptionally active between 5pm to 6pm on KESTREL AVENUE and our night firing positions. | |

Signed
O.C. 102 M.G. Coy.

Army Form C. 2118.

# WAR DIARY
## INTELLIGENCE SUMMARY of No 102 MG Coy.

(Erase heading not required.)

Instructions regarding War Diaries and Intelligence Summaries are contained in F. S. Regs., Part II. and the Staff Manual respectively. Title pages will be prepared in manuscript.

Vol XX

| Place | Date | Hour | Summary of Events and Information | Remarks and references to Appendices |
|---|---|---|---|---|
| | 12.11.17 | | Notification received from Brig.H.Q. that a section of No 102 M.G. Coy would be placed at disposal of the 16th Division for operations to be carried out by them on a date to be notified later, accordingly the two reserve Sub-teams of "D" Section relieved the 2 Gun teams of "C" Section in the line, and the whole of C Section stood by at Transchet lines awaiting further orders. | Ref sheets 57 B S. W. 1/20.000 |
| | 13.11.17 | 6 am | Indirect night fire carried out by our Guns on York Road 0.27.c.30.90 and Bottom Bridge 0.27.b.80.20 — 8300 Rounds expended. | |
| | 13.11.17 to 14.11.17 | 9 am | Enemy artillery showed some activity in valley towards GUEMAPPE with 77mm shells and his machine Guns were very active at evening stand-to but remained otherwise very quiet. Enemy aircraft were active on 12th but kept at a high altitude. | |
| | 13.11.17 to 14.11.17 | 6 am to 6 am | We fired 4000 rounds during the night on York Roads 0.27.c.30.90 and dugouts at 0.27.c.85.30. Enemy artillery quiet but his machine Guns very active during the night. | |
| | 14.11.17 | | In accordance with Brig.Gos instructions the Instructions in reserve relieved 4 Guns of No 240 M.G.Coy in left Battalion sector. | |

[signature]
O.C. 102 M.G. Coy.

# WAR DIARY
## INTELLIGENCE SUMMARY.
*(Erase heading not required.)*

Army Form C. 2118.

Of No 102 M.G. Coy.

| Place | Date | Hour | Summary of Events and Information | Remarks and references to Appendices |
|---|---|---|---|---|
| | 14.11.17 | 6am | Night firing carried out by our Machine Guns – 2000 Rounds on O.32.d.55.60 and 1000 Rounds on O.33.c.30.60. Enemy artillery more active in afternoon of 14th. | Ref Sheet 51.13.S.W. 1/20,000 |
| | 15.11.17 | 6am | | |
| | 15.11.17 to 16.11.17 | 6am | Usual night firing programme carried out, 2000 Rounds being fired on selected targets. Enemy artillery shelled SHIKKAR AVENUE & LION DUMP, and the usual shelling of our trenches, and a sniper was active against junction of BISON RESERVE, APE & IBIS TRENCHES. One enemy aeroplane was over our lines 11 am – 11.30 am 15th flying very high. | |
| | 16.11.17 to 17.11.17 | 6am | The whole 24 hours was very quiet. 3.30pm to 4.0pm enemy shelled RAKE TRENCH – 20-30-77mm shells, apparently at one of our working parties. We fired 4000 Rounds during the night on selected targets. Instructions received from D.M.G.O. "C" Section to proceed to barrage position under orders of D.M.G.O. 16th Division, and accordingly C section moved to 16 Div front. 2nd Lt Godfrething & 2nd Lt J.R. Hurtt (See Appendix I attached) | |

Sgd O/C 102 M.G. Coy.

Army Form C. 2118.

# WAR DIARY
## INTELLIGENCE SUMMARY.
(Erase heading not required).

of No 102 M.G. Coy

Vol XX

Instructions regarding War Diaries and Intelligence Summaries are contained in F.S. Regs., Part II. and the Staff Manual respectively. Title pages will be prepared in manuscript.

| Place | Date | Hour | Summary of Events and Information | Remarks and references to Appendices |
|---|---|---|---|---|
| | 17-11-17 | 6am to | Indirect fire carried out during the night on CAMBRAI ROAD 0.15.c 10.80 | Ref Map 51BSW |
| | 18-11-17 | 6am | and ST ROHART FACTORY | |
| | 18-11-17 | 6am | 3000 Rounds fired during night on enemy trenches and roads | |
| | 19-11-17 | 6am | Hostile Artillery normal | |
| | 19-11-17 | 6am to | 1500 Rounds fired intermittently throughout night on enemy Roads. | |
| | 20-11-17 | 6am | Enemy artillery quiet. | |
| | 20-11-17 | 6am | On account of the hostility of enemy withdrawing from present lines, no special instructions were issued to sections. On account of British advance, South in accordance with Bng.aid Pursuit scheme | |
| | | 12.30pm to 6.45pm | In accordance with instructions received from 3rd Division, we assisted in a Smoke operation carried out by 4th Division on left, by concentrating machine gun fire on STIRPGATS FACTORY, FACTORY TRENCH & WHISTLE TRENCH, 1700 Rounds being fired. Enemy artillery retaliated against nos 600, 600, and 60(?) m.g. Positions, but no material damage was done. | |
| | 21-11-17 | 4.45 5am | Enemy artillery put down a heavy barrage on ARRAS—CAMBRAI Road from 0.14.a 90.30 to 0.13.c 30.80 and a few 8" Shells near RAKE DUMP 0.14.a | |

[signature]
for O.C. 102 Machine Gun Coy.

# WAR DIARY
## INTELLIGENCE SUMMARY.
*(Erase heading not required.)*

of No 102 m. G. Coy.

Army Form C. 2118.

| Place | Date | Hour | Summary of Events and Information | Remarks and references to Appendices |
|---|---|---|---|---|
| | 21.11.17 | 6 am | No firing was done by us | Ref sheet 57 B 8 W S |
| | 22.11.17 | 6 am | At 5.30 am – 5.45 am 22nd enemy artillery again put down a heavy barrage on ARRAS–CAMBRAI ROAD. | |
| | 22.11.17 | | C Section returned to transport lines from 102 Division. A separate Report * of the operation carried out by this section is attached. | *Appendix I |
| | 22.11.17 | 2pm 2.45pm | In Co-operation with artillery concealed machine gun fire was carried out on suspected enemy trench mortars at O21A 15:70 & O21C 50 80. 7300 Rounds were fired in this shoot. | |
| | 22.11.17 23.11.17 | 6 am | 6000 Rounds were fired during night on suspected enemy m.gs and also Roads + tracks. At 5.20am. 23rd, enemy artillery again put down heavy barrage on ARRAS-CAMBRAI ROAD, which developed into desultory shelling till 5.45am – Hostile artillery also very active against BISON RESERVE, BUCK RESERVE and SHIKKAR AVENUE trenches. | |
| | 23.11.17 | 6 am | 13500 Rounds were fired at selected targets during the night. Enemy artillery shewed greatly increased activity during this period and retaliated at 6 am 7 m 23rd against all our night firing positions. A large number of RED, GREEN and ORANGE Rockets were sent up by the enemy 9 – 7.30 pm 23rd | |
| | 24.11.17 | 6 am | | |

H.H. Butler
O.C. 102 m.G. Coy

# WAR DIARY
## INTELLIGENCE SUMMARY.
*(Erase heading not required).*

Army Form C. 2118.

Vol _____ of No. 102 M.G. Coy.

| Place | Date | Hour | Summary of Events and Information | Remarks and references to Appendices |
|---|---|---|---|---|
| | 24-11-17 | 6 am | 400 Rounds fired during night on O.32.a, 92.60, O.32.d. 50.40. Enemy artillery fairly quiet. At 5.9's dropped near our No 6.1 Gun position at 1.30 pm but barrage nil. | |
| | 25-11-17 | 6 am | 6 Section in reserve relieved D section which returned to Triangular area in afternoon | |
| | 25-11-17 | 6 am | No firing was done by us during the night. Enemy artillery very active 8am - 9am. 25th. on our trenches from Couch River to GRRR'S-CAMBRAI ROAD. Large numbers of RED & GREEN Rockets were used by enemy 6pm - 7pm 25th — no apparent aid-ck followed. | |
| | 26-11-17 | 6 am | Orders received that gas would be used at 11.30 pm. 26th and that new machine guns would fire in cooperation on HILLTOP WORK & ST ROHART'S FACTORY. Owing to the rain the operation was cancelled, but the order was not received in time to cancel our fire orders, and 3000 Rounds were fired from 11.30pm to 12 midnight — enemy did not retaliate. | |
| | 27-11-17 | 6 am | | |
| | 27-11-17 | 8 am | Normal conditions resumed in accordance with Bge. orders. B Section in reserve relieved A Section in the line. | |
| | 28-11-17 | 6 am | Night firing was carried out during night on HILLSIDE WORK & Road Junction O.16.c.15.50 — 400 Rounds fired — only desultory shelling by enemy artillery. | |
| | 28-11-17 | 6 am | | |
| | 28-11-17 | 6 am | 11.30pm - 12 midnight gas was discharged by Special Coy. R.E. and our Guns fired 3300 Rounds against HILLSIDE, ST ROHART FACTORY and HILLTOP WORK in co-operation. | |
| | 29-11-17 | 6 am | Enemy artillery did not retaliate. | |

O.C. 102 M.G. Coy.

# WAR DIARY
## INTELLIGENCE SUMMARY.
*(Erase heading not required.)*

Army Form C. 2118.

Place: 102 M.G. Coy

| Date | Hour | Summary of Events and Information | Remarks and references to Appendices |
|---|---|---|---|
| 29/11/17 | | Instructions received from Bn. H.Q. that one section (4 guns) of no 240 M.G. Coy would relieve B Section on afft 1/12/17. It was already arranged for "A" section to relieve "B" on same day, the advance party of B section was sent to "C" section instead, and morning of 30th. | Ref Item 57 B 59. |
| 30/11/17 | | Orders received from Bn. H.Q. that the relief of B Section by section of no 240 M.G. Coy was cancelled, & was therefore re-arranged that "A" section would relieve "B" on afternoon of 1/12/17. During night of 29/30th 4500 were fired on selected targets. | |

H. O. 102 M.G. Coy.

# WAR DIARY

## INTELLIGENCE SUMMARY

102 M.G. Coy.

Ref Sheet 51.B.S.W

## APPENDIX I Vol XX

| Date | Hour | Summary of Events and Information | Remarks |
|---|---|---|---|
| 18/11/17 | | 6 Section 102 M.G. Coy. under Lt. Oftenburg were attached to 16th Division to co-operate with M.G. barrage for a minor operation. The position taken up by the Section was in POM ALLEY along Bank in T6.b. | |
| 20/11/17 | | Barrage opened at 6.20 a.m. on a line S. of FONTAINE LES CROISILLES and fire was continued at a diminishing rate until 7.50 a.m. when news received from On 20 16th Divn to continue fire till 8.10 a.m. 35000 Rounds were fired. At 3.25 p.m. 20% fire was again opened on a fresh barrage line - 3500 rounds fire. At 4.20 p.m. fire was again opened for half an hour - 8000 Rounds fired. From 10-11 p.m. the C of L line was lifted beyond the FONTAINE-LES-CROISILLES - BULLECOURT road to allow Infantry patrols to go out, but no SOS was received. J.H. Riddell 102 M.G. Coy | |

2/Lt O.C. 102 M.G. Coy

Army Form C. 2118.

# WAR DIARY
## or
## INTELLIGENCE SUMMARY.
### No. 102 M.G. Coy.
*(Erase heading not required.)*

| Place | Date | Hour | Summary of Events and Information | Remarks and references to Appendices |
|---|---|---|---|---|
| | | | Vul at Offinant J. | |
| | 2-11-17 | 5.15 a.m | Fire was opened see barr by means of R.M.G.O on a time line see fourteen fourth - 2300 Rounds were fired. | |
| | 2-11-17 | 6.30 am | Gun lot signal was observed and fire was opened and continued till 7.20 a.m — 5000 Rounds being fires. | |
| | 2-11-17 | 12.30 am | Slow fire was opened and kept up till dawn, when our S.O.S. was again observed and fire was continued for half an hour. 10,000 rounds were fired during this shoot. | |
| | | | Section returned to transport lines in afternoon. | |

R.H.R. R.M.G.
T/c. O.C. 102 M.G. Coy.

**WAR DIARY**
or
**INTELLIGENCE SUMMARY**
(Erase heading not required.) of **No. 102 M.G. Coy.**

Army Form C. 2118.

Vol XXI.

| Place | Date | Hour | Summary of Events and Information | Remarks and references to Appendices |
|---|---|---|---|---|
| | 1/12/17 | | "A" Section relieved "B" Section in left Bn sector on afternoon. "B" Section returning to Transport Lines. | Ref Sht 57/35.N |
| | 1/12/17 | 4.30pm to 6.30pm | 2000 Rounds were fired on TRIANGLE WOOD & HELL QUARRY O.32.d | |
| | | 7.0pm | Gas & Thermite was used by Division of our left, when enemy put down heavy barrage on our trenches till 8.0pm. | |
| | | | Enemy planes flew over our lines at 10.30am and 12.30pm. | |
| | 2-11-17 | 6am | We carried out mg fire on CHERRY BRIDGE O.32.C 96.45 from 6.30pm-7.30pm | |
| | | | 2000 rounds were fired. | |
| | 3-12-17 | 6am | Enemy artillery active during morning quietened down at 10.30am | |
| | | | Retaliated to our mg fire with M.G.s but no damage done. | |
| | 3-12-17 | 6am - 6am | 2000 Rounds fired on FORKED ROADS O.27.c.30.90 4.30pm-6.30pm | |
| | 4-12-17 | 6am | Enemy artillery & machine guns only slightly active | |

[signature]
OC 102 M.G. Coy.

# WAR DIARY
## INTELLIGENCE SUMMARY
*(Erase heading not required.)*

of 102 M.G. Coy.

Army Form C. 2118.

Vol XXI

| Place | Date | Hour | Summary of Events and Information | Remarks and references to Appendices |
|---|---|---|---|---|
| | 4-11-17 to 5-11-17 | 6am 6am | M.G. fire carried out against CHERISY — 1.30pm – 6.30pm 2000 Rounds fired. Enemy artillery active against trenches & Right Bn during day and left Bn late by night, a quantity of gas shells were also used. One of our guns in ROKE TRENCH was put out by shell splinter and was replaced by a reserve gun at Coy H.Q. | Ref Sheet 57.B.S.E. |
| | 5-11-17 to 6-11-17 | 9.13pm to 10.35pm 6am | From 9.13pm to 10.35pm we fired on enemy line from O.32.a.22.27 to O.32.c.20.80 in co-operation with artillery to cover an attempted raid on right Bde front by No 103 Inf Bde. 10,000 Rounds were fired during that shoot. |  |
| | 6-11-17 |  | In afternoon "B" Section relieved "C" Section in the line, "C" Section returning into Reserve at Transport Lines. |  |
| | 6-11-17 to 7-11-17 | 6am 6am | 3000 Rounds were fired during the night on O.W.a. 95 and scattered M.G. in St ROHARTS FACTORY. Usual desultory shelling of trenches by enemy artillery. WANCOURT was shelled intermittently 9/pm to midnight. Enemy aircraft were active during evening of 6 E. Bombs were dropped near own Coy H.Q. N16 & 2.B. at 8pm. |  |

O.C. 102 M.G. Coy.

# WAR DIARY
## or
## INTELLIGENCE SUMMARY.

Army Form C. 2118.

No 102 M.G. Coy.

| Place | Date | Hour | Summary of Events and Information | Remarks and references to Appendices |
|---|---|---|---|---|
| | | | Vol XXI. | |
| | 7.11.17 | 6am | Our M.G.'s fired 2000 rounds on CROSS ROADS O27c 30.90 — 6pm to 8.30pm. Desultory shelling from our trenches by day; quiet at night except for occasional bursts of machine gun fire. | Ref. Sheets 51B SyS. |
| | 8.11.17 | 6am | | |
| | 9.11.17 | 6am | Our machine guns fired against BOTTOM BROOK O27B.8.2. (2000 rounds) and ANGLE LANE O21a.3.1. to O21a.7.9. (1000 rounds) during the evening. Enemy artillery very active against ARRAS — CAMBRAI ROAD during afternoon. | |
| | 9.11.17 | 6am | We fired 2000 rounds against CROSS ROADS O32.6. 20.40 from 6am to 6am 10.K. Desultory shelling of trenches; none of our trenches appeared. | |
| | 10.11.17 | 6am | Information received of the probability of an attack by the enemy on morning of 11.G. on our front, precautionary measures taken. One section of No 240 M.G. Coy moved into line to strengthen our defence at GOEUL VALLEY. 8am to 1.0pm enemy steadily shelled battery positions to in AREAS N17a, B, 7C. at 1 p.m. shelling increased to salvoes of 3's, 4's in quick succession till 3.30pm. a no. of gas shells were included bye/Bho entered received direct hit from a heavy armour piercing shell. 1 but no casualties occurred; a number of gas shells fell on same area at 1.30am. O.K. | |

O.C. 102 M.G. Coy.

Army Form C. 2118.

# WAR DIARY
## or
## INTELLIGENCE SUMMARY.
(Erase heading not required.)

Instructions regarding War Diaries and Intelligence Summaries are contained in F. S. Regs., Part II. and the Staff Manual respectively. Title pages will be prepared in manuscript.

| Place | Date | Hour | Summary of Events and Information | Remarks and references to Appendices |
|---|---|---|---|---|
| | | | Vol XXI. | |
| | 10.12.17 | 6 am | 2000 Rounds M.G. fired on TRENCH & RIVER CROSSING O.32d 95.60. | Ref Sheet 51B S.W. |
| | 11.12.17 | 6 am | Platoon moved forward to NONCOURT in readiness in case of enemy attack | |
| | 11.12.17 | 6 am to 10 | M.G. fire carried out on CROSS ROADS O.32B 10.10. 1am to 2am. | |
| | 12.12.17 | 6 am | Hostile artillery active against left Battalion front during the night. | |
| | | 6.30am | Heavy bombardment opened on right of Divisional front, lasting till 7.30 am. At 7.15 am S.O.S. received by wire from 12 Slots and 12 West Yorks. 7.45 - 7's enemy planes active flying very low over our trenches and engaged by Rifle and machine gun fire. | |
| | 12.12.17 | 6 am | Night firing carried out on selected targets. 2000 Rounds. | |
| | 13.12.17 | 6 am | Enemy artillery quiet. | |
| | 14.12.17 | | Advance party of Nos 1 & 103 M.G. Coy was attached to each of guns for instruction. Night firing carried out on enemy communications. - 2000 Rounds. | |
| | 15.12.17 | | 102. M.G. Coy relieved by 103 M.G. Coy. On relief 102 M.G. Coy returned to Northumberland Camp and became in Divisional Reserve. | |
| | 16.12.17 | | May 6rod to 6.30 am & 8.30 am in accordance with Brigade orders. Cleaning up and G.O.S. Instruction | |
| | 17.12.17 | | One section wounded & Vickers Guns for anti aircraft purposes. | |

Army Form C. 2118.

# WAR DIARY
## — or —
## INTELLIGENCE SUMMARY.
(Erase heading not required.)

of No 102 M.G. Coy.

| Place | Date | Hour | Summary of Events and Information | Remarks and references to Appendices |
|---|---|---|---|---|
| | | | Vol XXI | Ref sheet 51B S.W. |
| | 18/12/17 | | Coy had dinner. Donations for this were received from Tynesiz Scottish Committee, Newcastle on Tyne, 34 Divisional Canteen fund, the remainder of the Cost being met by the Company's Canteen. | |
| | | | On account of motor lorries received from Bde HQ. that the Divisional Commander would inspect the whole Coy on 19th, the Concert arranges for after the dinner was postponed and cleaning up of all kit carried out instead. | |
| | 19/12/17 | | Company and transport inspected by Major General [Nicholson] Comdg. 34 Divn. followed by a short lecture by him to 90 to Officers and Senior NCO's. | |
| | 20/12/17 | | O.C. Coy reconnoitred Right Sector 34 Divn. front. | |
| | 21/12/17 | | Inspection of Coy by T.O. Section officers reconnoitred Right Sector 34 Divn. front. A no. 1. of each gun proceeded to the line, and were attached one to each gun of no 101 M.G. Coy. | |
| | 22/12/17 | | The Coy relieved 101 M.G. Coy on Right Sector 34 Divn. front with 16 Guns. The relief was completed without special incident. Indirect harassing fire was carried out during the night on targets as at O.26d 95.17 & indirect fixed firing pretty. | |

[signature]
for O/C 102 M.G. Coy.

Army Form C. 2118.

# WAR DIARY
## or
## INTELLIGENCE SUMMARY. of 102 M.G. Coy

(Erase heading not required.)

| Place | Date | Hour | Summary of Events and Information | Remarks and references to Appendices |
|---|---|---|---|---|
| | | | Vol XXI | Ref Sheet 51<u>B</u> SW |
| | 23/9/17 | 6 am | Enemy shelled area O.31.c central and Quarry intermittently during the day. No firing was done by us. | |
| | 24/9/17 | 6 am | 4000 Rounds fired by us on selected targets on enemy communications. Enemy shelled Quarry Dump intermittently with Gas Shells. | |
| | 25/9/17 | 6 am | | |
| | 25/9/17 | 6 am | Desultory shelling of CABLE & CURTAIN TRENCHES by enemy artillery with H.E.'s, also against SNIPE SUPPORT with trench Mortars. Visual signalling was observed in enemy's line, but nothing intelligent was picked up. | |
| | 26/9/17 | 6 am | No firing was done by us during the night. | |
| | 26/9/17 | 6 am | Enemy aircraft very busy during day — aeroplane firing on our front line trench with M.G. Enemy artillery quiet — a few shells fell on THE QUARRY. No firing was done by our machine guns. | |
| | 27/9/17 | 6 am | | |
| | 28/9/17 | 6 am | Enemy shelled MALLARD TRENCH with 5.9's. Enemy aircraft were active during the morning. Enemy machine guns traversed QUARRY DUMP intermittently during the night. | |
| | 29/9/17 | 6 am | 2750 rounds fired by our machine guns on selected targets during the night. | |

O.C. 102 M.G. Coy.

# WAR DIARY
## INTELLIGENCE SUMMARY. of No 102 H.Bty

Army Form C. 2118.

(Erase heading not required.)

| Place | Date | Hour | Summary of Events and Information | Remarks and references to Appendices |
|---|---|---|---|---|
| | | | Vol 221. | |
| | 28/12/17 | 6am | Enemy artillery shelled Quarry Dump intermittently | |
| | 29/12/17 | 6am | Scott available used actively during morning of 28th. Flying neither over our lines. Shells were engaged by our machine guns, too much fired. No firing was done during the night. | |
| | 30/12/17 | 6am | Enemy artillery very quiet. Very little done by us. The whole period passed very quietly. | |
| | 31/12/17 | 6am | Enemy artillery very quiet. No firing was done by our m.gs. | |
| | 1/1/18 | 6am | | |

Signed [signature]
for O.C. 102nd H Bty

**WAR DIARY**
**INTELLIGENCE SUMMARY**

of No 102 M.G Coy

Vol XXII

| Place | Date | Hour | Summary of Events and Information | Remarks and references to Appendices |
|---|---|---|---|---|
| | 1/1/18 | | No firing was done by us. Enemy artillery shelled Quarry Dump and rear areas intermittently during day. Much movement observed on enemy's lines. | Ref Sheet 57B S.W. |
| | 2/1/18 | | Enemy aircraft very active, a number of planes were engaged by our anti aircraft machine guns – 250 rounds being fired. PELICAN DUMP and rear areas intermittently shelled by enemy artillery. | |
| | 3/1/18 | | Enemy aircraft very active during morning. 350 rounds fired at same. Area O31C shelled by 4.2's and hostile Trench Mortars very active against our front line at O.31.d. central. 2000 Rounds were fired by our guns on selected targets during the night. | |
| | 4/1/18 | | Enemy shelled QUARRY DUMP, EGRET TRENCH and rear areas at intervals during the day. Harassing night fire carried out by our guns on enemy communications re Wood rounds fired. | |
| | 5/1/18 | | Enemy artillery quiet, but aircraft very active all day. 1000 Rounds fired by our anti aircraft guns. | |

J.F Whitley Lieut
OC 102 M.G. Coy.

Army Form C. 2118.

# WAR DIARY of 102 M.G. Coy

## INTELLIGENCE SUMMARY.

(Erase heading not required.)

Instructions regarding War Diaries and Intelligence Summaries are contained in F. S. Regs., Part II. and the Staff Manual respectively. Title pages will be prepared in manuscript.

| Place | Date | Hour | Summary of Events and Information | Remarks and references to Appendices |
|---|---|---|---|---|
| Vol XXII | 6/1/18 | | Intermittent shelling of EGRET TRENCH and area O31c.35.70. At 6 p.m. enemy put down a barrage on our front line at 6 p.m., and 250 rounds were fired on SOS lines by one forward gun. | Ref Sheet 51B S.W. |
| | 7/1/18 | | Desultory shelling of area O31c. Several Gas Shells fell on QUARRY DUMP. Enemy aircraft very active during the day. Enemy firing Camels out by our guns — 600 rounds fired on selected target. | |
| | 8/1/18 | | The whole day was exceptionally quiet. 150 rounds fired on O26d.40.90 | |
| | 9/1/18 | | The whole day was very quiet. Much individual movement was noticed in enemy lines especially on the HENDECOURT - DURY ROAD. 5000 rounds were fired on selected target | |
| | 10/1/18 | | Desultory shelling of QUARRY DUMP and SWIFT SUPPORT during the day. Movement on SUN QUARRY and UPTON WOOD observed. 900 rounds fired on O26.10.20. | |

R.A. Henderson Lieut
For O.C. 102 M.G. Coy

# WAR DIARY
## or
## INTELLIGENCE SUMMARY.
(Erase heading not required.)

Army Form C. 2118.

of 102 M.G. Coy.

| Place | Date | Hour | Summary of Events and Information | Remarks and references to Appendices |
|---|---|---|---|---|
| | | | Vol XXII | Ref sheet 51B S.W. |
| | 11/7/18 | | Desultory shelling of BURRAY DUMP and rear areas during the day. Much interval a have transport movement observed and enemy aircraft very active in the early part of the day. 1200 rounds fired in blocked target during the night. | |
| | 12/7/18 | | Intermittent shelling of BOOTHAM TRENCH and rear areas during the day. Harrassing night fire carried out by our guns 3000 rounds being fired. | |
| | 13/7/18 | | Very little enemy activity. 4.200 rounds were fired on enemy tracks and communication tracks | |
| | 14/7/18 | | Intermittent shelling of support lines during the day. Usual harrassing night fire carried out - 2000 rounds being fired. | |
| | 15/7/18 | | Very little activity. 5,600 rounds were fired during the night on enemy tracks and communication tracks. | |

Signed [signature]
for O.C. 102 M.G Coy.

# WAR DIARY
## INTELLIGENCE SUMMARY.
*(Erase heading not required.)*

of 102 M.G. Coy.

Army Form C. 2118.

| Place | Date | Hour | Summary of Events and Information | Remarks and references to Appendices |
|---|---|---|---|---|
| | 16/7/18 | | The whole day was exceptionally quiet. 3,500 rounds were fired on selected targets. | Ref. sheet 51 D S.W. |
| | 17/7/18 | | A very quiet day except for a few gun shells on EGRET TRENCH | |
| | 18/7/18 | | Very little activity. A few gas shells on QUARRY DUMP. 4000 rounds were fired on selected target. 102 M.G. Coy was relieved by 103 M.G. Coy. and went to HENIN CAMP. | |
| | 19/7/18 | | On relief 102 M.G. Coy. returned to Divisional Reserve. Day spent cleaning up and inspection in the afternoon | |
| | 20/7/18 | | Coy. provided working parties to assist R.E.'s in making dugouts etc. in the line. Work also commenced for reserve emplacements in Corps Defence line at HENINEL and WANCOURT | |
| | 21/7/18 | | Working parties & work on reserve emplacements continues | |

P. M. Hunting, Lieut.
2 i/c. 102 M.G. Coy.

Army Form C. 2118.

# WAR DIARY
## or
## INTELLIGENCE SUMMARY.
(Erase heading not required.)

Instructions regarding War Diaries and Intelligence Summaries are contained in F.S. Regs., Part II. and the Staff Manual respectively. Title pages will be prepared in manuscript.

of 102 M.G. Coy.

Vol XXII

| Place | Date | Hour | Summary of Events and Information | Remarks and references to Appendices |
|---|---|---|---|---|
| | 22/7/18 | | Working parties continued and work on reserve emplacements nearing completion | Ref sheet 15.18.5.W. |
| | 23/7/18 | | Work on reserve emplacements completed. Working parties to R.E.'s continued | |
| | 24/7/18 | | A test manning of reserve positions by A and C sections followed by an inspection by Divisional Staff Officers. | |
| | 25/7/18 | | Company moved to DURRON CAMP MORY and came under the orders D.M.G.O. H.Q. 40th Division. Enemy aircraft dropped 7 few bombs in the vicinity of the camp. | |
| | 26/7/18 | | Day spent cleaning of kit and inspection in the afternoon. | |
| | 27/7/18 | | Shooting of forward hit and gun kit under Section Officers A & B Sections. Finished working party to dig reserve emplacements under the arrangement of D.M.G.O. 40th Division. Enemy aircraft dropped bombs in the vicinity of the camp. | |

B.H. Lauderry Lieut
for O.C. 102 M.G. Coy

Army Form C. 2118.

# WAR DIARY
or
## INTELLIGENCE SUMMARY.
(Erase heading not required.)

| Place | Date | Hour | Summary of Events and Information | Remarks and references to Appendices |
|---|---|---|---|---|
| | | | Vol XXII | |
| | 28/7/18 | | C & D Sections paraded for cleaning kit and bath. Inspection of N° 60 & 61 in the afternoon. Enemy aircraft were very active during the night and many bombs were dropped. C & D Section continued work on emplacements. | |
| | 29/7/18 | | A & D Section paraded for cleaning kit and harness and continued work on emplacements at night. Enemy aircraft again over at night bombing. | |
| | 30/7/18 | | All rifles inspected and guns inspected by Armourer. Sections paraded for cleaning limbers at Transport Lines. Section Officers, Section Sgts & Corpals reconnoitred gun positions in the line by followed under the 6 Divn for drill. C & D Sections proceeded working party to complete work on emplacements. | |
| | 31/7/18 | | The enemy shelled ERVILLERS about 6.30 pm with long range HV Shells. An A.A.M. Gun was mounted ready for the defence of BURROW CAMP | |

J. P. [signature]
for O.C. 102 M.G.Coy.

www.ingramcontent.com/pod-product-compliance
Lightning Source LLC
Chambersburg PA
CBHW081529160426
43191CB00011B/1715